C000133947

SOCIA

MARKETING

2020

A BEGINNER GUIDE TO BECOMING A
SOCIAL MEDIA INFLUENCER

By Simon Kain

TABLE OF CONTENTS

INTRODUCTION

Social media marketing is the next big thing now. Social media has replaced traditional media marketing. It has replaced TV ads and newspaper ads. Every brand out there is looking for companies that will serve as their brand ambassador and help to promote their company. Brands are becoming increasingly aware that influencers are the driving force of marketing. They are acting as the middle ground between the brands and their potential customers. Everyone has one or more influencers that they are following. So, there is no better time than now to become a social media influencer.

The cool thing about being a social media influencer is that it's easy to do and you can still make money while doing it. Your educational background, your race, or your age doesn't limit you to becoming a social media influencer. You can become a social media influencer at the age of 14 years and still get brain deals and sponsorships. You can even become an influencer at the age of 10 and people around the world will be your followers. The only thing you need to do is to apply the tips written in this book, and in no time, you'll have millions of followers that you can make money from, even while you're sleeping.

So, this book is divided into 11 chapters. In chapter one, you'll learn how to grow your Instagram and get noticed by brands. In chapter two, you'll learn how to brand yourself on social media. In chapter three, you'll learn how to brand yourself on social media. In chapter four, you'll learn how to take pictures for social media. In chapter five, you'll learn some physiological tips on how to become a successful influencer. In Chapter Six, you'll learn how to start a YouTube channel. In chapter seven, you'll learn how to grow your Facebook fanbase. In chapter eight, you'll learn how to become famous on tik-tok. In chapter ten, you will learn how to get more twitter followers. In chapter eleven, you'll learn how to make money on social media. So, without wasting any more time, let's get started with chapter one.

CHAPTER 1

BECOME A SOCIAL MEDIA INFLUENCER AND WORK WITH BRANDS

When trying to become a social media influencer, the first thing you should remember is to pick your audience. If you do that then, people won't know what it is that you're all about, and they won't know what it is that they are following you for. You can't just wake up one morning and post-gym stuff and then the next day post super high-end fashion stuff. The gym stops and the fashion stuff won't go well. together.

CONSISTENCY

Consistency is the key to being an influencer. If you're not consistent enough, your followers won't look forward to seeing your stuff. You want your social media page to be real and authentic because people can tell if you're authentic, and if you're not authentic, they are not going to trust you. Post things that you actually use, wear, and that match your page aesthetics no whatever you are promoting. Also, you have to be consistent with whatever you are posting so that your followers and other brands will be willing to see your post. Now, this is not about getting huge followers. There are many influencers that have a low audience, but still get huge PR packages especially in the makeup niche. Makeup brands are trying to reach out to smaller audiences.

PICTURE QUALITY

Another thing that you need to consider when trying to become an influencer is your picture quality. Make sure that pictures of your posts are very clear. Now, this does not mean that you have to put scratches and filters on all your photos. People want to see you real in your photos, except maybe you were also in photography. Now, if you're using a filter on your photo, make sure that you stick to that. It doesn't make sense to have a page with blue photos everywhere, and all of a sudden, you start to post a black and white picture. When you put a picture that doesn't go with your other ones, just delete it. If you want to work with a certain brand, then post pictures that will make that brand to repost your picture and give you more exposure. If you want to work with a certain brand and you've emailed them, but they haven't gotten back to you, then buy their products. Take a picture that fits with the aesthetics and send it to them; maybe they will like it. On top of that, make sure that the picture is cool.

CONTACT BRANDS YOURSELF

Certain brands are not going to want to work with you if they don't see you wearing anything that you know that's theirs. There are so many brands that you can actually reach out to send you their products to promote. All you have to do is go on their Instagram and one DM. But DM them is going be a little bit hard because some companies don't go through their DMs. So, you can go to their website, scroll all the way down to the bottom and click on the contact button to send them an email. You can either send them by a direct PR email using the contact form, email them asking for their marketing managers' email, or get their PR email. You're going to send them a nice email introducing yourself in a very short way, with links to your Instagram page, YouTube page, or any other social media page on any of your social media platforms. So, introduce yourself and tell them why you love their brand with links to your work about their brand on your page. Then on the email, write your first and last name, with your shipping address, so that's going to make it easier for the company to send you their product. If it's a makeup brand, they'll just send you their product, without even needing to reply back to you.

LOOK LIKE THE COMPANY

Even if you have a small following, like a thousand followers, if every single picture is having a makeup look, when you contact the makeup company, they'll just send it to you or put you on their PR. They'll send you a care package to see what you'll do with the product. Then you can send them the links of the work you've done with their product. Then from there, they'll start working with you since you've proved yourself. As stated before, even if you don't have that big of a following, still use a lot of product tags on your post so that you get invited to these huge events, and get invited to expensive trips. So be consistent and tag everything that you're posting.

CLEAR PHOTOGRAPHY IS KEY

Make sure that your pictures are clear, not fuzzy, but clear. You have to understand the quality. Your pictures don't have to be like pictures taken by an HD photographer. You can take your pictures with your phone but make sure that it's nice. Clean it up a little bit; you can use your iPhones, don't use anything other than an iPhone. You can do cell photography because people just want to be like you in your pictures. They are getting over pictures with a magazine look. So, you don't need your photos to be all that professional except if you're someone like Mariana Huen. As stated before, you have to understand who you're targeting. Someone like Mariana can't just change like that and just start posting iPhone pictures. Her fans are going to be somewhat confused, because they like what she is doing now. They'll be like I followed you for that design, but am I following you for posting these iPhone quality pictures that you're posting.

POST AT THE RIGHT TIME

So, another thing you can do is to ask your audience what time they would like you to post. Right now, the best times to post are usually right after work, or during lunch hours when people are on their phone because they're just resting. You don't want to post in the morning time when people are getting ready for work. Post when people are interested in reading your post. Post consistently around 7-8pm, because you know for sure people are just sitting down with their phone. At that time, they are through with work and homework. So, you should post about pictures 90% of your social media post around 7-8pm and then sometimes post at random time. Sometimes a photo won't do good because you're posting it at the wrong time usually. The reason why you're doing this is that you want your followers to engage with you. You don't want them to just look at your photo and be like wow. You want them to like it, comment on it, and engage with you, so that you can engage with them back. You want to engage with your followers.

ENGAGE WITH YOUR FOLLOWERS

In your captions, ask them what they're doing this weekend or what they intend to do. You want to engage with your followers that way. Be personal thumb, because it shows you are trying to connect with people. You can do little stories, write something inspirational, or post about a thought that you're feeling, or better still, answer people's questions. Post something deeper that makes you connect better with your fans, more than just a picture. Interacting and having a deep connection with your followers is a super key. So, consistency and interacting with your followers is key. There's no reason why somebody should follow you if you're not going to engage with them. Unless you're like Kylie Jenner or Kardashian. Even those people still interact with their fans. They still comment on people's posts, especially on Twitter, all the time. But the thing is that just because you're aren't famous now on social media doesn't mean that you won't be famous someday. It's going to happen, but it's going to be a really tedious thing. So, you have to be patient with yourself.

GIVE IT TIME

Give it time, keep posting, build your audience, use hashtags too if you feel like you need to do. Almost everybody is using hashtag these days, but they help you to freakily gain followers easily. Even if your pictures are not doing well, leave it especially if it's a good picture, because if somebody goes on your page, they want to see as a bunch of content at the end of the day. When Brands go on your page and they want to see that you're consistently posting, and you're creating content. They don't just want to see 20 good pictures and then nothing. They want to see consistent hard work because hard work beats talent.

EMBRACE IMPERFECTION

It matters that if you have a whole production, consistency is the key. Don't post a YouTube video, that was hugely done with a bunch of professional lighting and camera; people don't want it. You want people or your audience to grow with you. Look at all these other influencers; they make videos of them making their first video. People can see that their video was cringing, but then they can see them sitting in million-dollar houses later, and that's motivating for them. Most people say I don't know how to make a video, or I don't know how to edit my videos, or I don't have a pro camera. The best advice for you at that moment is to learn and just get started. That's the key, start. Stop saying that you need a camera, or you need a light. It is okay if it's imperfect, especially if it's for YouTube. If you want to post your first YouTube video, post it. Nobody will care if you're embarrassed in it or not. Keep your first YouTube video safe so that you can see that transition from the beginning to where you're right now. You'll see that you're so much more confident and comfortable in front of the camera than you were before when you started. You'll see that in the beginning, you love to talk really fast, and you looked weird. So that's really it, you have to start from somewhere. So just remember not to give up and be consistent.

CHAPTER 2

GETTING NOTICED BY COMPANIES

In this section, we'll be talking about how to grow your social media and be potentially noticed by companies, whether its clothes, shoes, or makeup, and how you can stir up a whole social media movement. These tips will help to boost your following and your interaction. So, this section won't teach you how to get 50,000 subscribers overnight; no, these are real people that you don't buy from apps or anything like. No, these are real-life people. These tips will help you to grow your social media following for the most part. A lot of social media gurus don't like to share this information because they feel like if they do, more people are going to be doing it. To them, it's like a competition. But everyone can grow an Instagram following and get companies to send them stuff. So, there's enough of clothes companies, makeup companies, and companies looking to send stuff for everybody. So, there's no reason why you have to feel like it's a competition. You can do this whether you're a guy or girl. You can benefit from social media if you use it correctly. So, grab yourself a drink, grab yourself a straw, grab yourself whatever you want, because this section might be a little lengthy.

Be Consistency uploading

First thing we'll talk about is going to be consistency. Being consistent means having a little uploading, scheduled to go. For instance, during the week, you can post three times, or you can post every day if you're really about it. But you have to be consistent when it comes to posting. When you do that, you'll definitely see an improvement every time and you 'll gain more followers and more views to your Instagram account as opposed to waiting a week or two to post.

Search for what you should Post

Another thing that you should do when you post, is a search for what you should post. You can do a selfie, and then post an inspo picture, or quotes of the day, or an outfit of the day, or show some makeup product. So, don't always be posting selfies, selfies, selfies, or just outfit – outfit, outfits. Switch it up so that it won't be so repetitive, and people won't get tired of seeing just selfies.

Use A Specific Theme

They are some people that do IG layouts, like specifically a theme that they follow. It could be a picture quote, picture-picture-quote, and picture. And you know, you can follow that if you want to, because it looks really pretty and it's definitely more aesthetically pleasing.

Add meaning to your content

The third tip is to try and add meaning to your content. People must have a reason to follow you. There's a million beautiful banging body girls and guys on Instagram, so why would people choose you to follow. So, you have to decide. Are you're going to be showing off your style? Are you going to be showing off your makeup? Are you going to be showing off your food recipe or workout in your videos? Whatever you want to post, just turn it into content. For example, if you're going to do makeup, post the products that you use, so that if they like it, they can get it. So that way, you're bringing meaning to your picture, because not only is it a pretty picture, but another girl can grab the same lipstick or use the same products that you're using as a girl. For your clothes, you tell people where you buy them or the best seller, or the best discount price for them. Now, you're giving them a reason for them to follow you as opposed to these people that just post the pretty picture.

Pick your Content-Type

Another thing is to pick your content. This is going to be a little confusing for you if your Instagram is for personal use, but since you now know that you can actually make money from it, you want to start taking it more seriously. If in your content, you want to be doing makeup, ask yourself if you are going to be posting your outfits too, if you're then you're going to do a combination of the both. Whatever your content is, try to stick to it, don't sway from it, because then it gets a little kind of confusing for your followers. If you want to post pictures of you and your friend, do it in a way that it still goes with your clothing theme. If you have a pet or a cat that you're obsessed with, don't just make post picture of your make-up and then from nowhere post pictures of your cat. Post it in such a way that your cat inspired your make-up.

Make it cohesive, so maybe, posting about your cat inspiring your makeup will keep it still within the same vibe or the same theme of your Instagram account. Because you don't want to post your makeup outfit today and then post about your pet tomorrow, but you want your Instagram account to be more like a business. So, going off of your content picking your content, now when you want to do is make sure that you have quality content.

POST QUALITY CONTENT

So, by this, they are kind of narrowed it down to four themes.

USE A NICE BACKGROUND

So, the first one is to make sure that the background is nice. Secondly, make sure that the lighting is a bomb. Third, make sure that the picture is aesthetically pleasing; this goes for your makeup, this goes for your shoes, this also goes for your nails too.

Make sure that it's pretty and nice to look at. Also, make sure you have a good camera. If you're using a phone, then quality iPhones are the bomb. Or if you're serious and you want to invest in a camera, then do your research. So those four things will definitely bring quality into your pictures for Instagram. So, just to wrap up the beginning portion of what I just said, always be consistent with your pictures but, make sure it's not too repetitive. Find your niche content that you are going to focus on.

WHEN TO ACTUALLY POST

So, the first tip that I have for you guys is a when to actually post. Now post when you're normally on your phone. You can post when you wake up, you can post during your lunch break. Post when you get back from school or before you go to bed, those are the best times to post. So definitely, stick around those schedules when you're more likely to be on your phone is when other people are more likely to be on their phone too. So, therefore, more people will see your pictures and they'll hopefully like your pictures and increase your following, because if certain people follow your pictures, then you're more likely to come out in the recommended or in the search section of your Instagram for at least those times you're posting.

EDITING YOUR PHOTOS NICELY

The next tip is to have your pictures nicely edited. They're apps that you can use or filters that you can apply in your pictures. It's important if you have good quality content, but it's better if you can edit your pictures too.

Another tip is to tag your pictures with anything relevant to them. So, for sample, if you are a beauty influencer, tag the lipstick or the makeup that you're wearing. Post the store that you're buying your stuff from. Tag your accessories. tag your nail, polish, color, or tag anything relevant to your picture. The more people see your picture, the more the chance of them actually seeing your picture, and hopefully liking your picture, reading and your content, following your Instagram, and reaching out to you.

USE HASHTAGS ALWAYS

So, another big tip is to hashtag. Just like tagging, use hashtag on pretty much everything that's relevant to you or your picture. So, if in your picture, you're wearing an outfit, use hashtag beauty, hashtag cute outfit.

Hashtag basically everything, because people do look at hashtags to follow certain things on Instagram. If some girls are looking for which nails to fix, and they don't have a color or something, they might go into Instagram, spell out the hashtag, nail and check everybody's Instagram account with the resulting nail, and then they end up following the accounts that they like, because of a hashtag. So, a hashtag can lead someone to your account. So, don't underestimate using hashtags. Hashtag everything relevant to your picture or you.

For example, if it's just a selfie, you can hashtag whatever you won't like, but if it's a picture for your fans, use the relevant hashtags. Do you feel pretty? Hashtag pretty, hashtag Obama's book, hashtag blushes on fleeing. Hash-tag anything that is relevant to your picture or just you. If you're a Mexican, hashtag Latina, hashtag Mahika. Hashtag everything that you know is relevant to you or your picture. You don't just want to hashtag something because it's popular like Kim Kardashian. They'll just go to your picture and be like who is this.

If you just want to gain followers by hashtagging famous people, it won't work. Remember that your goal is to gain real followers on Instagram. So definitely don't buy fans or promote other people that you don't agree with on your page. Stick to hashtagging things, and even if it takes you a little bit longer, you're going to gain people that are actually going to follow you, and people that will be more likely to interact with you. You don't want people that are just going to just find you randomly on the internet with no idea who you are.

Do BRAND ENDORSEMENT FOR FREE

Another tip to get noticed by companies is to buy from their product, even if it's just one shirt, one pant, one skirt, or whatever you want to buy from them, do that. Wear that outfit as best as you can and then tag them, and hopefully, they'll see your picture and like it. If you apply what was mentioned earlier in this book, like having good lighting and posting quality content consistently into the companies' images, then you're more likely to get noticed. And they'll see that you're an actual supporter /customer. And if they like your ad, they might send you three hundred thousand dollars' worth of clothing to try it on.

Most little clothing stores, makeup stores, and shoe stores, for the most part in their bio, are using some recurrent hashtags. If you check on most fashion Instagram accounts, in most cases, you'll see that they have used a hashtag there. So, go to your Instagram page and use that same hashtags that these Instagram accounts used. So, take the time and do your research. Look at the accounts and see if they have a specific hashtag they want you to use, or a specific ad they want you to use. Check whether their featured pictures in search of their hashtags. Check out their ads. Incorporate their hashtags into your captions and that will definitely serve as a good way for them to reach out to you. They can just find or just discover your account like that, so you need to use their hashtag in your pictures.

We've talked about the tips and tricks to hopefully get noticed by other companies and boost your following. Now let's get realistic, and let's talk about the business side, or the reality, of Instagram and social media in general.

NUMBERS ARE IMPORTANT

I do not want to discourage you by any means, but the reality of social media life is that numbers are important to an extent. People that have more followers are definitely more likely to get noticed by more companies and bigger companies now since it is a numbers game, smaller companies or companies with smaller budgets will definitely reach out to people who have a smaller following and/or have the same amount of followers as the company. Because companies with smaller budgets don't have the thousands of dollars to pay for a huge Instagram famous person to promote their stuff, they'll reach out to a smaller Instagram account.

So, it is a numbers game, doesn't mean that you're completely left out of the game. If you don't have 100k followers yet, do not be discouraged. But you have to be realistic to yourself that bigger companies are definitely going to reach out to people that have more following. Smaller companies will actually send you their products even if you don't have a huge following on Instagram. Once you have around 6k or 7k followers on Instagram and about one to two thousand followers on YouTube and you're applying all the tips we've covered; companies will start sending you their products. They might find you on YouTube even if you only have two thousand followers to thousand five hundred followers at that point.

They'll still reach out to you if they believe in you. They might reach out to you and tell you that they really like your content and your personality. They might reach out to you because of the effort that you put into making your outfits cute. They'd like your content if it went along with their content. The fact that they can say that to you can really motivate you and make it stick with you. So, don't get discouraged with the numbers. It is a numbers game, but not everybody might hit it big with numbers.

PUT EXTRA EFFORT ON YOUR VIDEOS

With that being said, try as much as possible to put extra time and effort into your pictures, so that a company will want you to advertise their stuff. It's the same thing as putting time and effort into your post. If you display, for example, a make-up palette with bomb lighting in such a way that everyone can see every color in it when the palette is open. And then you also have music playing in the background and the video is so-mo so that viewers can get a good idea of what the product is. Because you're putting enough effort into making that product look bomb, more companies will keep sending you their stuff to promote, because they can see that you're taking your time to showcase their product.

But if somebody sends you a lipstick, and you just hold it up, and the background of your ad is plain in the back without any music playing, and you're also hanging awkwardly at the store, and you didn't use any cute hashtags or anything like that on the video, then they're less likely to reach out to you.

HELP BRANDS TO MAKE MORE MONEY

Brands are sending you hundreds of dollars' worth of clothes in hopes that it will generate sales for them. So, if they send you a hundred thousand dollars' worth of clothes or products, they're hoping that when you showcase it nicely, it'll generate a lot more worth in sells, maybe double that or triple times whatever they sent you. If it happens like that, then they're going to be sending you more stuff because their $100 turned into $500 investment with you really quick so they'll want to send you more. Of course, as stated before, the more followers you have, the more people will see your ad, and the more people will buy it. So again, it is a numbers game now I want to talk to you.

So realistically speaking, yes, it does take a long time to do your hair, or to do your makeup, or to pick out your outfits to wear, or even to pick a location that you'll take your pictures. It also takes time to edit your pictures. Pick the best time to post and tag it, and add a caption out of your hashtags. Yes, it takes a lot of time but you have to realistic about the time and effort that you're willing to put into your Instagram account. It's not only just snapping the picture or posting it. There's a little science behind the whole ordeal, so just be realistic about the time that it's going to take you. It's not impossible to do, and you can definitely manage your time and take advantage of certain things or certain situations to post your stuff. For instance, if you're going to eat breakfast in the morning, wake up a little bit earlier so that you can take the time to make your makeup and your outfit look cuter. When you go to have breakfast with your family, have them take a quick picture or a tangible thing that is super easy to do. Whatever you've planned for the day, just take your pictures and go on with your life. As explained, it does take a lot of time, and there's a said science behind the whole thing. The people that have over 100k or a million following on Instagram didn't just get up and take a picture and go on. They put in a lot of time and were consistent to grow their accounts. And in doing so now, they're able to make a living off of Instagram.

CHAPTER 3

How to brand yourself on Social Media

This section is basically about how to brand yourself on social media. The biggest thing right now is definitely Instagram. So, in this section, we'll be leaning a lot more towards Instagram, and alongside of course YouTube especially, if you are interested in starting a channel or learning how to grow a channel. We might also touch on Twitter, Facebook, and snapchat a little bit in this section.

When Instagram first came out, it was like the craziest thing, especially among college students. Everybody was off from Facebook and was now on Instagram. A lot of college students hadn't really picked up on Twitter a whole lot at that time. So, Instagram was the new thing. At that time, it was a perfect platform where people could share pictures.

Also, everybody wanted to see pictures and show off what they were doing. So, everybody gravitated towards it. At first, it was mostly for urban modeling and cross-promotion between the photographers. At that time, magazine models were busy doing cross-promotion. At that time, it was called a shout out for shout out. Everybody's was doing a shout out for shout out, of course, to gain more followers.

YOUR PAGE NAME

So, the first tip is about the name on your page. This is a very important thing. Because that's what people are going to remember, that's what people are going to first see. Before they even see your picture, comments, and all other stuff like that, they going to see your name. So, your name is very important on your social media page through no matter the number of accounts that you decide to have, whether it's from some certain apps or from some certain websites, especially on the simple normal ones that everybody uses like Instagram, Snapchat, Twitter, Facebook.

If you are going to have any social media account, you need to make sure that all your names are the same, and if the name is already taken, then you need to make it very similar to the real name. If you have two accounts on one platform, don't just delete one account and make and another one. Don't delete any of the two account but keep one account that will be separate from your main twitter page.

But from the beginning, make sure all your names are the same, and make sure that they're very close, because that will help people to be able to connect with and search you faster than ever. If you have a whole bunch of different names, on all your accounts, then it's going to be hard to keep up with.

YOUR AVATAR

Another tip that goes along with keeping the same name across the various platforms is using the same picture or the little avatar picture across all platforms. You need to make sure that it is the same on every site of course. Snapchat doesn't have a website or an avatar. The platform is a little bit different, but just make sure your name is the same on the platform.

YOUR BIO OR DESCRIPTION

Moving on to the bio, your page description is everything. So also keep it simple. Keep it clean, and also keep it unique to who you are and the statement that you're trying to get out to the world about yourself. If it's nothing that you really want to post in your bio, then don't force yourself to post it just to have a whole bunch of stuff on your profile.

If you have a location that you're specifically in, then put that in there, and you could maybe put a little pimp of your current location GPS. So, if you're in Miami, put it there because that's where you live. If you don't care to share your location, then don't put anything there. If you have another website, page, or something that you would like to link in the description, make sure you put that in the space that is available for it. For the description, try to keep it simple. Make it as unique as you are or whatever, it's that you are trying to just get out to people. So, in let order to people know a little description about yourself, write a little description about yourself.

YOUR PROFILE PICTURE

Your photos on Instagram, Twitter, and snapchat are very important. A lot of people will follow you first on Instagram, then they will brand out to the other social media accounts to follow you. Some of them will go as far as Twitter and as far as snap chat. And sometimes, they'll do the opposite way around, follow you on snap chat and twitter, and then follow you on Instagram. Some people might even follow you from Twitter, then follow them on Instagram, snapchat, and Facebook and vice versa; however, the case may be.

So, your Instagram pictures are very important if you want more followers and want your page to grow and your brand to grow. You need to brand yourself accordingly as far as having crisp, clean photos. There's not a whole book to jump on your page if you are trying to promote yourself. Your page is like your personal social account. So, if you just want to grow your pages and have more followers on them, then you need to take more pictures and stay active on those accounts.

If you have a twitter account, and you have like 4,000 followers, but you're not engaging with your fans, and your engagements are really in the dumps because you don't tweet a lot, then you won't have a lot of fans. It can be quite hard to since there's no immediate response on Twitter, but Twitter is a really good platform to just even browse and stay up on the news, so you want to engage with your fans there too.

Now for your Instagram pictures, you need to make sure you have a nice clean background. If you're going to take pictures of yourself, then take it in such a way to make your brand grow. If you're into photography, then, of course, you may take a picture of your camera, or have a person take a picture of you using your camera, or whatever the case may be. But the pictures are very important. Right now, videos aren't as important as the photos on social media, especially if you aren't going to be talking much in the videos. If you're not showing much about your brand or who you are, then there's no point in using videos. You don't need to have any videos on Instagram, especially if you're a heavy snap chatter. If at all you want to show your face in a video on Instagram, then you should utilize the Instagram live feature. The Instagram live is amazing and it's a great way for you to interact with your followers and for them to interact with you back. You can get a lot of new followers if you par venture pops up on the explore page.

So, they're just so many different ways to get your brand out there and get your name out. Now with snapchat, you might need to be snapping light, even if it's 100 seconds. You can even make your snaps just over ten seconds or even like two to three seconds, depending on and if I had text in the picture or not. Then try to also do a lot of cross-promotion on your social media accounts too. So, for instance, if you do a YouTube video, put it on your Instagram story and in your snapchat too, and also attach the link of the video in your Instagram story. Of course, snapchat have the slide book feature self that is available up there, they currently took the swipe up feature off of YouTube, so you can use it to promote your page. Now on Facebook, you can cross-promote there too because you can forward a video over from YouTube to Facebook. Even on Twitter, you can do the same thing.

So, branding yourself is all about putting a lot of effort into it. It also means putting in a lot of love and just being patient and somewhat just letting yourself grow. Also, growing your Instagram page, Twitter, Snap Chat, Facebook all those use tags and locations. Those are very vital to growing your page because if people see that you're in a certain location, they'll click on the location and see what other pictures are up there. Also, if they're in a certain location, they'll click the hashtags to see who's up there, just because you do happen to have a picture that catches their eyes.

And then they might even end up following you so, which is so important.

USING HASHTAGS

Hashtags, too, are so important. A lot of people use different hashtags to get their posts seen by many people. So, if you're using the same hashtag that everyone is using, like the hashtag, Instagram, then the chances of somebody seeing your photo will be slim, just because of the number of people that use the hashtags. It also depends on how frequently they use it, and how many likes that photo gets because the most popular photos are going to be at the top of the screen. Twitter also works almost the same way with snap chat. You can tag your location on it, however it's just a little bit too unsure of doing that, because you may be in a specific area with your location is on, and you may not want people to know where you are.

USING TAGS

Tagging everything is mostly for Instagram, and tagging goes for both hashtags and tagging brands in your actual photos. It is even more important in the beauty industry to use hashtags. Therefore, the number one tip is to use tags. Now when growing your following, you won't be having a consistent number of followers every day; you might grow three hundred thousand followers in a year, but that does not mean that you will have 1000 followers every day.

Sometimes you might have 300 followers; some other days you might have 500 followers. Also some days you have 600 followers, while some other days you have even have 1000 followers. But then you will have those crazy days, where a brand will repost you, and those are the days where you will gain 2000, 3000, 5000 or 7000 followers.

Now hashtags work because other influencers do check out those hashtags. There are some days that you'll get lucky and end up in the top hashtags for a single tag, which contains the top 9 photos of any hashtags, and that is when you will see your engagements literally doubling. Because not only do other influencers check those hashtags but brands do as well, you literally get 10 hashtags. But only the first 10 are going to show up in the actual tags; anything after that is useless. So, if you are in the beauty niche, try to tag makeup brands. Now, most brands do check their hashtags, so it's always a smart idea to go on a brand page and look in the description to see if they have any strange cookie hashtags. Also, you have to be tagging brands consistently, especially if you are too nervous to email brands or reach out to them directly. Full tagging brands are the easiest way to network.

That is how you will end up on a major PR brand's list. It is so simple, but so many people don't do it and this is how to brand out from the make-up that you have been wearing to try another brand if you're in the makeup niche. That is also how brands will find your work for the repost, opportunities or sponsor post or affiliate works. You have to let them know that you exist.

Choosing a name

Brand yourself especially if you are in the preliminary stage of creating your account. You have a choice of whether to use your real name or a catchy name because you haven't gotten any following. While branding yourself, you have to decide whether you want to use your real name or a catchy name. If you want to have many following on Instagram, YouTube, and other social media platforms, then you should go by a catchy name because a catchy name is a cool, memorable, and easy to spell. Going by your initial name or your legal name can work out well, especially if you are working in the beauty community. But if you want to grow a large following, then it is better that you go with a username, especially on Instagram.

On YouTube, your username is very important because that is what goes by directly underneath your video. This is a very important decision, and most people don't think about it very much, when they are getting started on social media. So, you can choose to go by your real name or choose to go by a catchy name, it's all based on your personal preferences, but surely a catchy name will do better than a real name. However, do not go for a long name, a name that is difficult to spell, or a name that includes numbers in it. You can choose to go by your legal name if it is short, catchy, and easy to spell or just find yourself a username, which is easy to spell and say vocally. If you are the primary stages of trying to build a social media following this tip is going to be very important for you.

USE LONG DESCRIPTIONS

It is going to be difficult at first, because when your description is really long, you will be thinking that you are spamming people, and that those people are not ready to read all of your descriptions. But the truth is that they do read all your descriptions.

INVEST IN YOURSELF

Invest in equipment or knowledge. Trying to be a social media influencer online is very difficult because social media space is so saturated as so many people are trying to do it. Brands are not going to repost blurry photos; there are so many options and there are other people who are capturing meticulous photography with amazing lighting and perfect cropping that have sharp crepes and really shows them off. With a blurry photo, you're not going to get a report. You're not going to also get followers. Even on YouTube, nobody has time to sit them and watch a video that is less than 360p.

However, this doesn't mean that you have to go out and buy a $6000 camera. It does not also mean that you have to buy a $1000 red light on Amazon. But you can shoot better pictures and create better videos for free if you have the knowledge for it. So, you have to learn how to use the tools that you have to create better photos and videos. You don't have to go out and buy some boxes and an external microphone and an ambient light. You can use your iPhone to take a video. This is as easy as going around your house and finding a place that has the best natural light. You can sit in front of a window and record with your iPhone and it will look amazing. So many top-quality influencers are literally using their phones rather than a digital camera, and that is because they know how to manipulate light, and they know how to edit.

EDIT YOUR PHOTOS

Now when it comes to editing your photos, you don't have to pay $200 for Photoshop; you can use free apps to do it. You can use the app called free app to do it, the setup is so cheap, and it works fine. So, you can take photos on your iPhone, stand in front of a window and edit them using a free app we like face tune and after light. And within two hours, you can have Instagram worthy photos that a brand can definitely repost. But you can't be lazy on this stuff, you have to figure this stuff out. Of course, it is easy if you can go out and buy the professional equipment, but if you don't have money to buy the professional equipment, you can do everything for free, and still have good quality photos on your social media.

DO IT FOR THE RIGHT REASONS

Some people don't know that social media influencers do exist. Some other people don't know that one can make a living out of social media, even though they're always on social media. Now there's nothing wrong with trying to be a social media influencer, but you have to be doing it for the right reasons. There are so many guys and girls out there that don't know what they are doing. That is, they are clueless about the social media game. While the ones that have some clue about what they are doing are just doing it for the money and for the brand trips, so they make their followers lose faith in them immediately because they take every brand digit that is given to them without any quality filter and vetting.

People can spot a fake social media influencer from afar, especially in a field that is already saturated. Most people can spot authenticity. Becoming a social media influencer is not an easy job by any means. You have to really love it. You are self-employed and you have to find a lot of your own opportunities and it is 100% inherent in self-motivation, because nobody is going to be kicking your ass and tell you what to do. If you are lazy and you feel like you don't have to work at all because you have some savings with you or because you're starting to get some brand deals on social media and you have little to no responsibilities, then your growth will stop. And for months at a time, you won't be able to gain any followers again, because people will tell that you are not loving what you are doing, and you are not putting any effort into it. There are so many people trying to do exactly what you are trying to do on the internet, but they are not many people who genuinely really love working on the internet.

BE PATIENT

This may sound silly, but don't be biased. If you are reading this book, then it shows that you really want to become a social media influencer more than anything. And the easy way to succeed on this might be just to buy followers so that brands will notice and take you seriously. The truth is that they wouldn't. Having high subscribers or followers count doesn't matter anymore. The thing that matters most is views and engagement. It doesn't make sense if you have 200000 followers, and you're only getting 200 likes on your photos. Other brands and other influencers will know if you have bought followers or not. So, buying followers will just ruin your image on the internet, and people won't honestly trust you. If you spend $100 to gain one hundred thousand followers and you never get to engage with them, neither do they get to engage with you, then you are not an influencer. Because the fun part about being an influencer is to able to engage with people and have them engaging with you too.

CHAPTER 4

HOW TO TAKE PICTURES FOR SOCIAL MEDIA

In this section, you will learn how to take pictures for your social media. It looks really easy, but most people that try to take pictures for their social media for their first time find it difficult to do. Many things that come into play when taking pictures for your social media and making them look nice and professional. These tips in this section will help you even if you have never taken a professional photo before.

Now you can use these photo tips even if you don't have a camera to use. You can use your iPhone 8 camera. You don't need an expensive camera or super-expensive HD quality type of video camera to take professional photos for your social media. So, here are some of the tips that will help you to take professional images.

LIGHTING

Lighting is the most important aspect of having a nice picture. Lighting can make or break your photo. The best lighting to take pictures in is golden light. Most Photographers love it. Golden light is the light that you have on the sunset and on the sunrise. So, the golden light is the light that basically sees when the sun is rising. It is normally right in front of you and looks goldish and warm. So, when taking your photo, you want that one goldish light to hit you right in front of your face. If the lighting is too bright or too low, it will create a shadow or a shade on your face, and it will not look good.

You can also take pictures on the sunshade where the sun is not that direct; that is if you're taking your pictures between 12:00 and 3 noon. The shade will make the picture to look a bit diffused. However, you have to be careful when taking pictures in the shade with your iPhone, because the iPhone can make it have more contrast and look darker than it actually is. So, if you can, just try to take pictures with the Golden shade. If you are inside, then try to take pictures in front of a window, because the window will give you the best lighting since it is the lighting that comes directly at you.

ANGLE

This is another very important point tip in having a very nice photo. So, in this case, you might want to get somebody who knows your angle like your friend, my mother, boyfriend, brother, sister, cousin, or even a random person on the street that knows your angle. If the person does not know your angle, you can actually describe it for that person. You could say something like, if you haven't guessed before, I'm actually small. Many people think I am really tall. I just look tall in pictures, because I take my picture from the ground.

If you are a small person and you want to really look tall in your photograph, then let the person that is taking you the picture snap it from your legs up to your head. It will make you have longer legs, and you will look a lot taller. Another good tip, if you are small, is to take the picture from your hip area up to your head.

One thing to avoid when taking pictures is the tourist picture trap. We've all been there and we have all done that, but it is not good to keep falling in that trap if you want to grow your social media account and gain more following. The tourist picture trap is when you take pictures in a nice area where you have a nice view. And then you stand at that spot, and let the person in front of you to just take your picture from your front to whatever is behind you. This is what it's called the tourist trap picture because it does not look artistic, especially if there's more than one person in the picture. Of course, there is nothing wrong with taking group pictures.

But if you want your picture to look a little bit more artistic, then try to take them from a different angle. If you're at Brooklyn Bridge in New York, instead of just taking the picture plainly in front of you, with everything behind you, you can ask the person that is taking you the picture to take the picture from the angle rather than right in front of you. That way, you'll be able an artistic depth of field and also make the picture look less flat and make it have more dynamics. Always try to play around with angles and viewpoints in your photos, even if you are at home you can try to go outside and see what looks good.

LOCATION

When it comes to location, you can get creative with it. There is an unlimited amount of locations that you can take pictures in. You can choose to take your pictures inside or you can choose to take your pictures outside, it is really up to you. The most important thing when taking your pictures is the vibe you want to give up in your pictures.

Do you like blue walls behind you or white views? Then you can try to take a picture in front of an entrance to get that nice majestic look in your photo. One great spot to take pictures in, you like that edgy, sporty look vibe is an empty parking lot. Some people might say that a parking lot is ugly, but a parking lot can really give that great street style wipe to your pictures. So, taking pictures in an empty parking lot is great. Also, try to avoid places that are crowded because you don't want to have people appearing at the background in your picture. You just want to look good in your picture. If other people somehow appear in the background, then it is good to photoshop them out. Another great location to take a picture is a flower wall. Right now, there are flowers for every color that you can take pictures in front of them.

Colors

The next step to taking a great photo is color. You want your Instagram account to have reoccurring colors that is, if you're going for a color theme. However, you don't have to stress too much over the color theme or try so hard to keep the same color theme all over your Instagram all the time. If you want your picture to look really nice and colorful, then it's good to incorporate three colors that you like in every picture. If you like white, blue, and Brown, then try to incorporate them in all your photos. If you want to go for a colorful theme, then you can use flashy colors in your photos.

Choosing your color theme is going to totally depend on your personal style and how you want to express yourself creatively. Your Instagram page is where you want to really express your view vibe, your mood and what you stand for. If you are creative, then Instagram can just be an amazing outlet for you. You can also get inspiration from other people. But try as much as possible to use your own style in your own picture.

Accessories

The next is accessories. Most people forget that they can dress up their pictures with accessories. Accessories can make a huge difference in your pictures. They help to put everything together and make your picture look interesting and nice. They also help to give you a picture of something to look at, and it's aesthetically pleasing to look at.

One of the things that you can wear in your picture is glasses, clothing-wise, you can also wear bags and nice-looking shoes for your photographs. You can also decide to add food as an accessory to your photo, which means that you can take pictures while you're eating. You can also decide to add a book or newspaper flowers and roses into your field pictures if you can.

Drinks can also add a vibe to your picture, but it's a Starbucks drink or a Courtney polythene cocktail stop just get creative with using different types of accessories. You might even go as far as using blankets, pillows, teddy bears, cars, and dogs in your photos. Even cars and mopeds can act as an accessory to give up that vibe that you want to give out.

TAKING PHOTOS WITH AN IPHONE TRIPOD AND A CAMERA

When you're shooting your photos, it's a lot easier to have someone taking your photos for you because that person is going to help you get the correct lighting and angle for your photo. But if you don't have anyone that is going to take pictures for you, then you can use an iPhone tripod to take photos yourself. The iPhone phone tripod cost about 10 bucks on Amazon. You can either have the tripod make your phone vertical or horizontal. The next thing that you have to do is open up your camera and figure out the angle that you want to take your photo in.

Now it can be difficult to take the picture because you have to keep coming back to see what the picture looks like. So, in place of that, you can get a Bluetooth remote camera controller. You can buy it on Amazon, you can link it up to your phone with Bluetooth, or you can just turn it on. So, when you click the button on the remote controller, it will take a picture. It is so much easier than setting a timer and keep running back and forth to your phone.

CAMERA

Now, as for the camera, if you want to buy a camera for shooting photos on your social media, then buy a Canon 70D, which has a Canon 10 to 18mm lens; the camera is wide, and it captures the whole shot of your body. You can also choose to use a Sigma 30mm 1.4-lens camera. Now you can download the Canon app on your phone so that you can see what you are taking on your phone when you're standing in front of the camera. So, you can set the camera on your timer two high-speed continuous shooting so that it can take a bunch of pictures at once, and you can move it around to get cool shots.

HOW TO EDIT YOUR PHOTOS

Now that you have known how to take pictures with your camera and with your iPhone, it is time for us to talk about editing. So many apps exist that you can use to edit your pictures. If you have a computer, you can purchase the Lightroom app for editing your photos.

LIGHTROOM APP

The lightroom app is one of the best picture editing photos out there. It is somewhat pricey, but if you want to take your Instagram account to the next level, then it is something that you might want to invest in. So, first, import all the pictures that you edit into Lightroom. On the lightroom app, go into the preset options and use the aspen ovanrd presets. Presets are so amazing on Lightroom, they just make your photos look amazing, warm, and orange.

And they can add a lot of vibes to your pictures. Now depending on the lighting, you can raise up the exposure or make it look a little bit lighter. Then you can go over to the color mixer, pick the orange option, and take down the saturation a little bit. Now you can also play around with the hue to make the sky look bluish.

Another thing that you can do in Lightroom is to see the before and after of your photo. The thing is to try to keep it simple. Do not go overboard and make the editing look fake.

After that, you can export the photo to your computer desktop and send it to your iPhone so that you can post it.

Smartphone photo editing

Another app that you can use if you don't have a laptop is the after app, it is a smartphone app. If you want a vintage look, you can click the dusty option on the app to give the photo that vintage look. You can even add flames to your photo with the app. The photo also highlights which is cool. After you have everything edited, everything, you can use an app called preview up to load your Instagram and plan out what you want to post. The after app makes you see how your post will look like in your Instagram feed. As stated before, try to keep everything simple posting Instagram is a process that actually takes a long time to edit pictures.

How to vlog in public

When it comes to vlogging in public, it can get really hard. Sometimes it is difficult to get the confidence to do it. So, here are some of the best tips for vlogging in public. In this section, we are going to be talking about vlogging in public. These tips that will be sharing in this section will help you to be bold and be confident when you are trying to vlog in public.

Just do it

The first tip to vlog successfully in public is just to do it. When you first start vlogging, it is going to be uncomfortable. It is going to be a little bit awkward. It won't be natural, so of course, you are going to feel a little bit awkward, so the only way for you to get over it and become comfortable doing it is just to do it. You have to do it repeatedly to the point where it just becomes natural and super instinct for you. So, you have to know that the more you try it, the more it the easier it becomes for you.

PEOPLE ARE NOT THINKING ABOUT YOU

People don't think or care about you as much as you think they do. Most times, you think that people are watching you or obsessing about you. But the truth and the reality are that they are busy with their own life. They are thinking about their own stuff. Even if they see you doing weird things, they might just look at you for a while, and then they are going to be off to the next thing. So, you have to really keep it in your mind that no one really cares about you and no one is really thinking about you, and they're not really upset about you. They have too much going on in their own lives.

BE BOLD

Rather than being shy about vlogging in public, try to be bold, be loud, and be confident. One way to do this is instead of you to start vlogging in public, instead start vlogging in your room so that before you get around people or in public, you are already talking loud full. So instead of people to be looking at you weird, they're going to be curious about what you are doing. And people might even ask about what you are doing, and who knows, you might get a brand sponsorship right on that spot.

They might come and ask you whether you are creating a video for YouTube rather than looking at you from afar and thinking that you're doing something weird. So being bold is a great way to start getting more comfortable. Even if you are in the front of family members, try to raise your voice and be bold and just say hey, what's up. Because if you don't talk loud on your blog, then you are not going to demonstrate confidence. So, make it obvious that you are vlogging in public. Even if it is coming off as rude, you just have no choice but to go for it. Just be so confident of breaking through the noise.

KEEP IT SHORT

What this means is that you shouldn't create long-winded videos. Don't have this huge conversation with yourself before you start creating the videos. Just get on the camera on and just say what you need to say and then just turn off the camera. When you keep it short, it is going to be punchier and it is going to be more comfortable, especially if you're in public

YOUR AUDIENCE AND COMMUNITY TAKE PRIORITY

Your audience and your community are very important to you. If people looking at you are strangers, your community and your audience are no strangers to you.

So, you have to realize that you have an audience, and you have a community that you are creating content for, and they are the most important in your life, so you have to be bold. You have to be confident. You have to be putting out content. That is why you are capturing all the events that you go to. Whatever the thing, you're capturing in your vlog, you want your subscribers to see the best of You and have the best information. Just remember that your audience and your community is the most important. Don't let the judgment and the perception of strangers affect the content that you intend to deliver to your audience.

CHAPTER 5

PHYSIOLOGICAL TIPS TO BE A SUCCESSFUL INFLUENCER

You don't need a certificate to become successful in social media. You don't need a doctorate bachelor's degree, Ph.D., or schedule to become successful social media. You only need to know about the ethics and guidelines that you need to abide by when it comes to working with brands and your followers.

BE SOCIALLY AWARE

The first thing that you had to take into consideration is to be socially aware. You have to know that somebody out there is willing to watch you and follow you. The next thing that you want to do is to make mistakes and make friends, and you have to do it with an open mind. In the piano world, the piano teachers do record their student play to help the students to learn about their technique style and mistakes and the emotions of what they are playing. The same thing happens in social media. Sometimes on social media, we get so busy that we don't have the time to self-reflect.

We just look at our social media posts and judge what is performing well numerically. However, it more than just seeing impressions on your social media posts online. It is more about the impression that you are making in-person and how you're communicating it. So, make friends with people online, because there are no degrees, or classroom social media where you can just find someone like you. On social media, there are different varieties of people, so you have to mingle with different people. And if the relationship doesn't work out, then be fine with it.

MAKE MISTAKES NOW

It is very important when you're starting social media to make mistakes fast. Don't fall into the trap of trying to make everything to be perfect. Don't fall into the trap of trying to make your lighting to be perfect. Don't try to make the way that you speak look perfect. The beauty of becoming a star is to show yourself to the world. People want to see you grow. People want to see you transition from pumpkin to a carriage.

They want to see you transition a stressful moment to becoming a diva. People want to see you go from having no makeup on your face to having full makeup on your face. There are a lot of people that love to watch that process. This doesn't just apply to your face, but from your career and from your personal standpoint. People want to see you grow. They want to see you win, so it's ok if you are vulnerable. So, if you are too scared that you're going to mess up or you don't have the right equipment, then you shouldn't.

MAKE DECISIONS FOR THE LONG TERM

This means that you should set long-term goals. When you are starting on social media, it's easy for you to be jaded about money and self-worth, but if you want to work with brands and big companies, then you have to be able to provide value to them. It's not just about money. You also have to consider your subscribers and your followers. So, you want to make sure that you are creating an organic and honest relationship with both you, and the brand, and in turn, you and your followers. Because if you just focus on the relationship between you and the brand and you're just worried about money, then that shows that you are selfish, and you don't care much about your fans. You are not genuine with them.

Also, if you see a brand and you like that brand, buy their products, buy both premier and their professional products at the same time. Try to support the brand as much as you can, and eventually they will invite you to go to the first-ever brand trip that you will ever attend. Then, later on, they'll feature you in different campaigns and ads for their product. So, it's not just going to benefit your fans; it is also going to benefits the relationship between you and the brand.

Whenever you have or see products that you love, share them with your followers.

DIFFERENTIATE BETWEEN BUSINESS AND PERSONAL

You have to know your place when it comes to separating between your personal stuff and business together because when you're on social media, these things can be interchanged together through setting unclear expectations on social media. So, you have to be able to differentiate between your personal stuff and your business. If someone on your followership just doesn't like what you are doing or you feel that person hates you, try as much as possible to keep things professional. You just have to be professional and be kind of proactive and genuine as much as you can. So that you'll be able to get the benefits of being an influencer. If you want your family members to work for you, then you have to make sure that that person knows about social media and knows about your craft very well. You don't want to bring someone that you will have to be training and be showing them every little thing.

When it comes to your parents, please try to keep them out of this social media game, because they are probably old fashion, they don't know more about social media. Even if they do, they can't even seem to get along with it.

BE MAGNETIC

If you want to be an influencer, you have to be positive and magnetic. Don't try to be fake. Try to talk about the positives in your life. Don't force yourself to do something that you don't want to. You just want to be magnetic because that is what will make you star. Even if you are tired, you don't to be seen as been tired. Because saying that you are tired is just a turn off for most people, and it is not inspirational for many people. Always try to talk about what you're working on. Always try to talk about what you are doing.   Be engaged. Also, try to go to events. Because that is the time for you to learn what's working for other influencers and know how you apply it to your Instagram account and social media.

ASK QUESTIONS

You want to be asking questions as much as you can. However, you don't need to ask too many questions. Try to ask a few questions and ask them at the right time, so that you don't end up annoying the person. Because not everyone is going to be that open or is going to be willing to even open up them to you. So, you have to consider if it is the appropriate time to ask those questions. To truly connect with people, you have to shift from asking them how their day is going to asking them what really makes them trust people and how do they balance their life? Just smiling and saying hello can make a big difference. Always make it a point to say hello first.

YOU DON'T NEED TO BE IN THE UNITED STATES

Try to be focused and creative. Even if you grew up without any cable or internet connection in your childhood, you could still be successful on social media. In fact, staying away from social media sometimes can allow you to have less noise and more canvas to create. Sometimes try to go out to look at or listen to music and just watch other people's videos. Because at times social media can really be cloudy and noisy, which will stop you from creating and growing as an artist?

Yes, it can be helpful to be in the United States. But you are better at creating content from your country. So, you don't really have to be in the city where you have to go to an event after the event. When you go to an event, you will spend so much time out of your day. Because you will spend time to prepare, you will spend on the plane or train. You will also spend time at the event. You'll spend time when coming back home.

Also, when you are at these events, you might want to go out to eat with people or go out to the club around those events. And before you know it, you have spent 7 to 8 hours of your time hanging out with people when you could be at home creating a video that would have gotten a million views. The only time you should start traveling around or moving out of your country is when you have created so much content for your YouTube and your Instagram and you are already working with brands. At that time, you will be traveling for Grammy awards. You will also be travelling to be in the news and to be in the daily pop. But this will come later on after you have gotten millions of fans.

GIVE PEOPLE SOMETHING TO REMEMBER YOU FOR

When it comes to living your mark as an influencer, whether online or offline. Try to create a magnetic personality. Create a story. Make something personal so that people will have something to remember you. Remembrance is reciprocal so, whenever you meet people, try to create a story in your head to try to remember them.

BE ORGANIC WHEN IT COMES TO NETWORKING

When you're going to networking events, you have to know that it's not just about kissing somebody's ass or just saying hi to somebody. Networking is about creating a relationship. When you are an influencer, you have to know who the person that you are networking with is. You have to be on the spectrum of what you know them for. You have to ask different things and information about them. You have to know what they do every day and where they are from, trying to be a natural interviewer.

CHAPTER 6

How to start a YouTube channel for beginners

This section will break down the very beginner steps on how to start your YouTube channel and what exactly goes into that process. Having a YouTube channel will be great for you if you have something that you are very passionate about and want to share with people. Having a YouTube channel will also be great for you if you just want to connect with people in general, or maybe you want to make YouTube become your full-time career and earn a full-time living from it. By the time you have enough subscribers from YouTube, you'll be able to support yourself with the earnings from the channel which is a really fun way to earn a living.

So, here are the steps that you need to follow to start a successful YouTube channel.

Choose a topic

The first step of starting your own successful YouTube channel is to choose a topic for your channel to choose a topic that you are passionate about. Because if you want to have a successful YouTube channel, you will have to make so many videos that are mostly focused around one central topic. So, you have to make sure that you choose something that you can talk over and over about it. If you are trying to decide a topic that you should choose for your channel, then you should go ahead and look at all the channels that make videos around all the topics that you are passionate about and see how much demand there is for all the topics that you are passionate about.

You will find out that some topics are more popular on YouTube than others, and if you want to become a big-time influencer on YouTube, then it is better that you choose a topic that has enough people interested in it. Now it is ok if your channel is about multiple different things, especially if they are coherent together, but when you're first starting out, it's better to keep your channel focused and only talk about few topics so that you can really start to attract people that are going to be interested in every video that you create.

GET CLEAR ON WHO WILL WATCH YOUR VIDEOS AND WHY

You have to become clear about who your subscribers are going to be and what value they are going to get out of watching your videos. People are only going to watch your videos and subscribe to your channel if there is something that they're getting out of your channel, even if that something is entertaining or just pure relief from boredom. But you have to figure out who these people are going to be and why they will want to watch your videos, so that you can decide which videos are really appealing to them, and the videos that will continue to appeal, interest and engage them.

BRAINSTORM 100 VIDEO IDEAS

The next step is for you to brainstorm 100 video ideas. Now you don't need to need to create 100 video ideas, but for your own benefit, you should think of 100 potential video ideas to create. The reason why you create 100 video ideas is so that you will never feel like you don't have a topic to make your next video about. You will always have this whole bank of ideas with you. And then the second reason why you should brain storm hundred ideas are that if you just create videos with the only first few ideas that come to your mind, then those videos might be really good, but you will not have something to compare those videos to. But instead, if you come up with 100 video ideas, then you can choose the very best of those ideas to create a video about. So after you have come up with a hundred video ideas, then you want to try and narrow it down to just the 10 top ideas that you are most excited about and that you can see that based on research, the most popular ideas that most people are really interested in watching.

CHOOSE YOUR EQUIPMENT'S

The next step about having a popular YouTube channel is to choose some equipment. Now, as stated before, you don't need to really have fancy equipment to create a YouTube video; you can get started with your iPhone. Even if you don't have an iPhone, a smartphone that was made a couple of years ago can still be used to create an ok video quality on YouTube, and phones tend to have really quality audio as well.

So, you won't even really need a microphone when you're starting out. The thing that you have to keep in mind is that if you have a camera that does not have a good quality, then you might need to get a lighting material because lighting has a very dramatic impact on the quality of your videos. The more lights that you can get on your face the better your videos will look, and that will really impact the number of people that will subscribe to your channel when they watch your YouTube videos. So, there are a lot of fancy lighting systems that you can use and some of them are expensive.

If you are doing this on a budget, then as stated before, try to go for a natural light that is sitting in front of a window and let the light hit your face. Then the other way is to go to Wal-Mart and buy a light that was made for a living room that has multiple bulbs that you can point in different ways, which is called a tree light. The cool thing is that you can go to the section where they are selling bulbs and buy bulbs that have cool colors, the highest watt of that light bulb.

The three lights will cost about $2, while the light bulbs will cost about $15 for a pack of three. So for about $35, you can get a light that will have to give your photos a really natural look and make them bright. And once you get a couple of those, your videos will look so much brighter and have better quality.

DECIDE ON YOUR CREATING AND UPLOADING SCHEDULE

This is the next step that you need to decide on when you are trying to create a successful YouTube channel, don't just decide on which days you are going to upload, but also decide on when you're going to get those videos filmed. So that you can put it on your calendar but make sure that you create a YouTube video every single week. So, for the best results, try to upload once every single week. Uploading two or three times can be great if it isn't compromising the quality of your videos. Just make sure that you're not focusing on the quantity over the quality of your videos.

You need to be consistent with your creating schedule, but you don't want to create plenty videos, because quality does matter, especially if you're trying to stand out in a place that is really competitive like YouTube. of course, you can batch film your videos and film three or four videos once or twice a month to get all your videos filmed, but when you're first starting out it's better to film once per week. Because you are going to improve the quality of your videos a lot faster by creating the videos one after the other, and you'll get more comfortable on camera and more quickly because you'll be practicing more regularly.

CREATE YOUR YOUTUBE CHANNEL

The next step is to actually create your YouTube channel. YouTube actually makes this very easy for you to do, especially if you already have a Gmail account. You can just basically login on your Gmail account on YouTube, and then click on the register button to set up your YouTube channel. It is simple to do, which makes it easy for anyone to do. Once your YouTube channel is actually set up, make sure that you don't skip the next step.

DESIGN A BANNER AND WRITE YOUR CHANNEL DESCRIPTION

These two things are really going to make your channel look a little bit more professional. Professionalism may not be what you're exactly searching for on YouTube, but nevertheless, having a channel description and a new well-designed banner will make it looks like you are a lot more serious about what you are doing. So that after someone watches some of your videos, they can click on your videos and see that you are actually making videos regularly and you're actually committed to it, which will make them eventually hit the subscribe button. Also, your channel description and your banner allow you to add your information.

FILM YOUR FIRST VIDEO

Now don't overthink this, it's probably going to be a little bit awkward if you have never done it before. But that is what everyone goes through and that is one of the costs of starting your YouTube channel and getting it off the ground. There are so many good things that can come from having your own YouTube channel, so you just have to bite the bullet and film your first video. After you film that video, then you should do the next step.

EDIT YOUR VIDEO AND DESIGN YOUR THUMBNAIL

So, after you have filmed your video, you should proceed to edit your video and create a thumbnail for it. Chances are where you create the first video, you are going to make a few mistakes so you need to pop your video footage into some editing program. They're great editing options out there like iMovie on Mac, or Windows Movie Makers on windows, and then there are so many other editing options like Adobe Premiere Pro. However, it doesn't matter so much about which program you choose when you're first starting out, the thing is that you shouldn't choose an editing program that is overly complex and confusing.

Try to choose a simple editing program that you can pop your footage into that program and then just cut out any mistakes. And then you can add a title tag at the beginning of the video to tell exactly what the video is all about. Then after you have edited the video, you can take a screenshot from the video to use as a thumbnail, or you can use another photograph or design a graphic for yourself as the thumbnail. You can use a free program to create a thumbnail for your video like canvass, or photo aura, or you can use an image editing program like Adobe Photoshop or illustrator to help create your thumbnail. The main thing that you want to keep in mind when you're creating your video thumbnail, is the thumbnail needs to be as eye-catching as possible; make it really clear about what the video is all about.

UPLOAD YOUR FIRST VIDEO

The best time to upload your videos is first thing in the morning to give people the most time to watch them during the day especially if you are on the west coast. But this doesn't mean that you cannot upload your videos at different times of the day. So there isn't any particular set time that you can upload your video, but generally, it is best to upload at the same time all the time, because with each video that you upload you are going to start attracting people that are watching videos around the time that you're uploading it. So, if you are uploading videos at 6am in the morning, and then later you start uploading videos at 4pm, then all the people that normally watch your videos in the morning by 6am will not be able to see your videos at 4 in the afternoon. So, try to be consistent with uploading your videos.

LIKE COMMENT AND SHARE

Try to give your videos as much boost as you can, because when you're first starting out, every little tiny bit of promotion that you can do for the video will really help it. This really means that you should watch the video yourself, hit the like button, and then leave a comment as yourself asking other people to give a comment, and then you should share that video with everyone you can. Share the video with your friends on Facebook. You should share the video on Twitter, and on your Instagram page. Tell people that you just made your first YouTube video, and shoot out an email to some friends and family and ask them if they can possibly help you out by watching your video and hitting the like button.

This is because every little bit of promotion will help you when you're just starting out. There is a huge difference between a video with two views and a video with 30 views, even though the 30 views aren't that much, but at least it shows that some people are interested in the video. And the more views that videos have, the more likely people are to click on the video and watch it, because of something called social proof. Social proof makes us think that if other people are doing something, then that thing must be a cool thing to do.

STAY CONSISTENT

The next tip is to stay consistent. When you start your channel, everything might look new, bright, shining and exciting and you will be motivated to continue, but as time goes on especially when you have put out five or ten videos, and you do not see very much growth, you might feel discouraged and feel like quitting or giving up on your YouTube channel. But one thing you have to know is that it will take a little bit of time to grow a YouTube channel. No YouTube channel that has ever-consistently put out YouTube videos, with interesting, eye-catching thumbnails consistently and did not start seeing a consistent significant growth within the first 6 to 12 months.

So, it is not going to take forever to grow on YouTube but you have to stay consistent. You need to keep uploading videos every single week. You need to keep improving your quality with every single video if you want to see that growth. If you want to turn this into your career and you want to reach more people and turn this into a full-time hobby, no matter what your YouTube video goals are, if you really want to achieve them, then you really have to stay consistent.

HOW MUCH MONEY CAN YOU MAKE ON YOUTUBE?

If you are reading this book, then you have probably heard of famous YouTubers making money off the platform. Now, the question is, can you make money on YouTube no matter where you live in the world? Well, in this section, we will be breaking some stats and data that will show you if you can make money on YouTube or not.

YouTubers are now being called videopreneur, especially YouTubers that are making a living by creating videos. And it's crazy with what is happening on YouTube these days. YouTube is more like a secret society for videopreneurs. An example of a YouTuber that has made a lot of money from YouTube on the internet is slime Queen, who is 23 years old. She was able to turn her one-time hobby, which is posting DIY slime videos on YouTube into a full-time career. Now she has gone from waitressing to making millions off YouTube.

Also, a report from Google found out that YouTube partners are now making more than six figures per day from YouTube. So recently, on the Creator blog, YouTube has stated that many creators on YouTube are making more than six figures every year.

This means that tens of thousands of individuals are making more than six figures on YouTube per month, and it is becoming mainstream. We are leaving in the era of YouTube income right now. There are thousands of creators on

YouTube generating over seven figures per month on the platform, and there are over 10000 YouTubers generating six figures on YouTube. Then, there are hundreds of thousands of YouTube creators that are generating about five figures per year on YouTube.

Now you don't have to make a full-time living On YouTube, you could make something as small as $35000 per year or even ten thousand dollars per year, which is cool since you are simply doing what you love, and still make money from your other side incomes. So, if you want to take a passion and generate money from it, then YouTube income is a great way to go.

Now all money we mentioned above that YouTube creators are making is based on YouTube ads, which is about 10 to 20% of what most YouTube creators make in total on YouTube. So, there is a crazy video revolution that is happening online right now. People are becoming millionaires by creating YouTube videos. Then those people that are not millionaires on YouTube have been able to make a full living out of YouTube without even having hundred, thousands, or millions of subscribers. So, here are some of the ways that you can make money from Google AdSense.

GOOGLE ADSENSE

So, if you're interested in doing with the first source of making revenue from your YouTube, especially, then the first source of revenue is YouTube AdSense. This is where the money comes directly from YouTube and get deposited directly into your bank account. You don't really have to do anything to make this money. It is a source of passive income. You just need to monetize your videos, and all you just need to do is to receive your money. Now the reason why most people go for this source of revenue on YouTube is that first, it seems like it's a very easy to source of revenue to make because you don't really have to do anything nor interact with anyone.

You can do it all by yourself if you just produce enough quality content, and there is no third-party involved. It is very tempting to follow this route. Most people that are not even You Tubers think that You Tubers make a lot of money through Google AdSense. But this is not all the case. Most of the top You Tubers do not rely on this source of income; in fact, some of them have stated that their YouTube ad revenue is not even 3% or 5% of the money that they make on YouTube.

However, this is a very minimal way to make money compared to the other ways that we will be talking about this section because it's a very great way to make passive income from YouTube. It gives you a way to pay your bills and earn a few bucks per month.

However, this shouldn't be your primary source of income and it should not be something that you rely on if you really want to make this as a career. If you are trying to make your channel monetizable for AdSense, then the first step that you should follow is to make your content very searchable. Look for the keywords that are going viral and topics that are trending, and then create videos around those topics. Also, create videos for topics that are going to be watched month after month. Because with Google Adsense, the more content you have, the more checks you are going to get.

So, if you upload like 20 videos and 3 of those videos are still getting viewers and are still being searched for in the search engine, then you are going to have a baseline for how much you are going to be paid month after month. So, the best way to make your videos such that both your subscribers and your non-subscribers will be able to watch the videos month after month is to make the video searchable.

Some of the videos that are consistently watched on YouTube are weight loss videos, tattoo videos, hair fail videos, makeup videos, music videos, and art videos. These are videos that people are consistently looking up every month. People are going to be constantly searching how to lose x amount of weight in x amount of days, so when people search that keyword, and you have a video around that keyword, then that video is going to pop up, which will be able to create a steady income for you month after month with AdSense.

Some people are generating about six figures per year with a small subscriber count on YouTube, not from YouTube ads, but other income streams. So Adsense is one way to make money off YouTube, but there are other ways that you can make money on YouTube without having an AdSense account.

BECOME AN INFLUENCER

This is one of the best ways to make money on social media. There are third-party sites that host influencers and brands. All you do with these sites is to make a profile and link all your social media account; your Instagram, your Twitter and your Facebook account, with your YouTube, and then set your prices for certain campaigns. Also, you can look through each brand on the platform to know what their budget is, and how much they're willing to spend to run a campaign, and then you can send them a letter or a proposal of how much, you would like to be paid for a particular campaign. There are some sites that allows you to list how much you charge for an Instagram post or for a YouTube video, and then brands will be able to reach out to you.

So, in this method, you can set your own rates and remove the middleman and start making money from your social media following. You can do it as a small influencer even if you have less than 20 thousand followers, brands will still be willing to work with you. Now the reason why you should do follow this route on making money as a social media influencer when you have a small following is that not only will you learn how to make money, you will also learn some ins and out about the industry. For instance, you will learn how to send a small invoice. You will learn how to negotiate with brands. You will learn how to write a business email proposal and you will learn how to set your rates. You also learn how to edit it and shoot videos and content.

DO AFFILIATE NETWORKING

This is another way to make money from your social media following. This means that you can work with one brand for a long time, and that brand will support you 100%, but if you have to follow this route on making money to your social media following, then you have to believe in the brand 100%. You have to believe in the product 100%, and you have to be willing to use and try the company's product. When you are an affiliate, you are literally putting yourself out there and you are literally making yourself a monetary representative for that brand, so if they do something a little bit shady, it will affect you too.

So, you have to be ready to stand by the product 100% if you are going to be an affiliate with the company, because you are making money with the company too. The best thing about being an affiliate is that there is no cap to how much you can make. If you really want to hustle and make it big time, you will keep spreading the links of the products that you are promoting every single day on all your social media platforms. You can even go outside to promote your social media, create a business card with your affiliate link there, and go and be slipping it under people's doors.

There is no end to how much you can hustle through this method. The only thing that you have to do is to find a company that you will do this for. You can even do this for Amazon or for uber. However, the best thing to do is to should find smaller companies that agree to have you on board with them regardless of your numbers. Then go online and look up how to write a professional business email and then send them a business email stating your numbers and your analytics. And most times, they will be more than happy to have you as a representative for the brand. One thing that you have to note is that you should not accept any free product in exchange for a post on a video or review except if you are obsessed with the product, and you won't care if you buy it anyway.

And you have to love the product, because it is amazing and you also love the company and want to talk about it. This method is less stressful and it's a great way to make money with your social media following if you really love a company and you are really enthusiastic about that company. It's a great way to make money without putting yourself under pressure to talk about things. This is a better way to make money than waiting for a brand or a company to send you a product free so that you will make a video on it in 2 weeks.

As stated before, do not accept any free products in exchange for a post just because you are in haste to make money. You don't really need to be paid to post a video about a company's products. So, don't accept to promote any company's product that you don't love especially when you're a smaller influencer, because it can be really tempting to do.

EMAIL BRANDS

You can send an email to companies like, "Hi my name is duke. I have over 15,000 followers on Instagram and my rate is $500 per post; would you like to work with me." Most times, they will respond and sometimes they will get back to you and say that they don't have enough budget. A lot of times, they will get back to you and tell you that they will gladly pay $250 per post. Or they might even say that the price sounds great, and they are willing to work with you. Brands are learning these days that influencers are invaluable marketing tools. Influencers are so hot right now, and so many brands are willing to work with you, just as you are willing to work with them.

CHAPTER 7

HOW TO CREATE BECOME AN INFLUENCER ON FACEBOOK

The most important thing that you have to create if you want to become an influencer on Facebook is a Facebook page. A Facebook page will allow you to brand yourself and gain more following. So, in this section, you'll learn how to create a Facebook fan page to brand yourself.

CREATE A FACEBOOK PAGE

Before you create a Facebook page, you need to have your own personal Facebook account. After you have done that, you can click on create, and then click on create a page. After that, you'll be shown two choices to choose whether you are a business or a brand, or you are a community or public figure. If you choose the option, business, or brand, you'll be brought up with the option to choose a page name and the category for that page.

But in this case, we are going to choose a community or public figure page, because actually, you want to become an influence on Facebook. So, click on the community or public figure option to get started button, and then you'll be brought with two options to enter your page name and your category. After you click the continue button, your page will then be created.

Add your Facebook page picture

You can add your Facebook page picture and Add it to your page. You can take a photo, or you can upload a photo to your page. Now as a public figure, you must use a picture of yourself with a white background. After that, you can add a cover to your page. The cover can be either a photo or a video. If you're adding a picture, make sure that the picture is about 800 * 312 pixels, then after that click, the save button. After you have added the cover photo, you can then add a call to the action button. You can choose the kind of button that you want to have. You can create a call to action for people to have a booking with you, or for people to contact you, learn more about you, download your app, or shop with you. If you want to send people to a website, then you have to select the create a booking with me, and then click on the link to a website, and then put the website there.

Edit your Page settings

After that, you can go into your page settings and can edit a lot of information about your page. For your visitor's post, you can choose to allow visitors on the page to publish the post, or you can disable post by other people on the page. It is better to disable the post by other people's option; if not, a lot of people be able to spam things on your page. So, it is better that you turn that off because you want to use your page to broadcast the things that you created. After that, you can go to your messages option to allow people to contact your page privately. The next one is the tagging ability option to allow others to tag photos and videos published by your page since it is free publicity. Also, choose the option to allow other people and all those pages to tag your page.

After that, go to your page info settings and write a description about your page, and when you are finished, click on the save changes and then enter your phone number and your website if you have one. If your page does not have a website you can click on the option my page doesn't have a website. If your page doesn't have an email, then you can also select the option not to put any email there; after that, save the changes. Then, go to the messaging options you can use the return key to send messages, you can also choose to allow the show in messages greeting option. This option will allow Facebook to automatically send a greeting so that people will see it the first time when they try to have a conversation with you on messenger. And then, if you want to activate the automated responses, you can do that by going to the response assistant option. And on that response assistant option, you can choose to turn on the instant reply on.

After that, you can go to the template and tab option to choose the ordering of your tab. They are also page rules settings that you can activate on the Facebook page. So if you have a really big page, then you can choose to allow other people to help manage your page, and then they can respond to comments so you can assign other people to be an admin commentator, editor, or a moderator and advertiser, or an analyst on your page.

Create your Facebook Post

After that, the next thing is to create your first Facebook page post. You can also choose to share your Facebook page post on your Facebook profile. If you click on the share button, you can decide to add your own story to it. After you have done that, then you should put something out on your page so that your page will not be totally empty; it could be a simple image or a blog post.

Customize your Facebook page URL

Now Facebook page gives you the option to customize your page URL, so if you go to your page to see the option to create page username, but you need to have at least 25 likes another for you to create your own custom page username. So, to get some likes on your page, you can invite some of your friends to like it. Facebook allows you to invite your friends from another platform to follow your page. So, after you have like 25 likes on your page, then you can create your own username. If you have 1000 friends and invite all of them, then you are more likely to get more than 100 likes. Which is good to help you get your first username.

GET MORE FACEBOOK LIKES

 After that is all sorted, then you want to go to the next step to get more Facebook page likes. The best way is to join other targeted Facebook groups. Running a Facebook ad is still the easiest way to get Facebook likes and it is surprisingly cheap. However, if you don't have some bucks to run add to your page, then joining other targeted Facebook groups is the simplest technique that you can use to get targeted likes for free.

Follow Groups related to Your Niche

All you have to do is to find groups that are related to your niche that allow groups to join them. All you have to do is to hover around the join button and it will tell you whether pages can be allowed to join the group or not. If pages are allowed to join the group, then click on the join button to select your page and join the group, after that then join other groups with your page and then wait for a little while to be accepted into each group. Once you are accepted into each of the groups, then it's time to post some content into each one. Now you can do this by another sharing posts from your page to the group, which will display a link back to your page below it, or you can just upload your own image directly into the group. Often you will start to get some likes on your page instantly once people start to find your page inside of your group. Now after sometime, when people have liked your post in the group, you can then invite them to like your page. Facebook will send a notification to those people prompting them to like your page. It takes some time and some effort to do this, but if you are posting the same content, then you can get some likes without spending any money on advertisement. This makes it a good way to get your page of the ground, especially if you're on a budget, and you don't have the money for ads yet. However, you have to be cautious not to post too much inside of any of the group, or you will come across as a spammer. Try to spread your post across many different groups. Now it's time to move on to the next step.

Run Facebook Ads

The next step is to buy some ads. This is by far the best and the quickest way to get a ton of hyper-targeted likes on your page. You don't really have to be a Facebook ad expert to create a Facebook ad. It is strictly easy to do. All you need to do is to head over to ads manager, and click the create button to create a new ad, then under consideration, select the engagement option, and click on page likes which will tell Facebook that your main goal on the ad is to get some likes to your page.

After that, try to create a campaign name, you can name your campaign anything since no one is going to see it. Next, the hit continues the next to create a name for your ad.

Again, nobody is going to see the name for your ad, so it doesn't matter what it is after that, select your Facebook page as the Facebook page that you want to promote now.

The next thing that you want to do is to select the country that you are going to be targeting. The United States happens to be the cheapest country to target for Facebook likes. So, when starting out, you can select the United States to get a cheap cost per click, and then you can dive into other countries later on.

After that, choose the age and gender that you want to like your page. If your page is something that is heavily targeted towards a certain age or gender, then it is a good idea for you to become more specific with the age and the gender option. But if your page topic is very general and appeals to a lot of people, then you can just leave it as it is so that Facebook will don't do the work to find out who in particular is responding the most to your ads and show your ads to them.

However, you want to make sure that the age maximum on your ad is 65; you don't want people that are 70 years or above or people that are your grandparents to be following you on social media, so let the maximum be 65 years. If you select people that are above 18 years, then you are probably selecting people that have credit cards and can be able to buy any products that you recommend on your page.

After that, choose your language. If your language is English, then choose English. After that, you can type the interest that you want to target. It's so simple to type in the main keywords that you want into the targeting section. When you type in the keyword, you'll be able to see your potential reach at the corner. The potential reach is the number of people on Facebook that will match your criteria and will see your ad. If your reach isn't quite that big, then you can always try adding more targeted interest. You can add keywords that are closely targeted to your main keywords.

In the main section, you want to make sure that you exclude people that have already liked your page, because you don't want to make waste money running ads to people that have already liked your page. After that, you need to choose your placement. You can choose to set your placement to automatic. Automatic placements mean that your ad will be shown on both desktop and mobile devices. But it is much better to target mobile devices because the likes that you will get from mobile will be cheaper, and most people are always on their mobile devices, so there is no need to choose the desktop option.

Next is to set a budget. When you're starting out, choose a very small daily budget. You can choose from 1 to 5 dollars a day, that is all you need. After that, click on the continue button and then upload an image for your ad. Now you can choose to use the Facebook built-in image feature to find pictures for your ad, there are many good images on a Facebook library that you can use, or you can decide to upload your own image. Once you pick your image, you can then preview it to make sure that it is looking good and just like your profile image. You want to make sure that the image on your ad is eye-catching and it tells people what your page is all about and the image looks good on a smaller resolution. After that, add some text to your ad to prompt the user to like the page. Just write something simple and straight to the point like, "hit the like button, if you like this page."

After that, scroll down and hit the confirm button to complete creating your ad. Then you need to wait for Facebook to approve your ad, which usually happens very fast. Sometimes it only takes a couple of minutes for your ad to get approved and running. Once you have been approved, you should start to see likes coming in almost immediately. Normally, you will see that you are getting likes to your page for about 4 cents per like, which is pretty decent considering that you are not doing anything on the ads. The cool thing about the Facebook ad is that the people that like your page are highly targeted. There are some campaigns that you will run for your page that will cost about 1 cent per like for a long period. However, the cost per result will depend on many factors, which include your niche, your ad image, and your targeting settings. You can also average the cost per like down even further going to your ad-option after the ad has been running for a while.

The Next thing to do is to click on the Facebook post with the comments button, then from there, you can view all the people that have clicked on the like button on your ad, but didn't like your page. So, what you can do is to go through all of them and invite them to like your page. Usually, they're a lot of people that will like your ad, but won't like your page. So, this is a good way for you to really get more results for your money when it comes to running ads for your page. This stuff is simple, it is not rocket science, all you need to do is to turn off some ads when you want to, and you will see just how simple it is to run an ad on Facebook.

Post Some Engaging content on your Page

The next step to get likes to your Facebook is to post out some engaging content on your page; this is after you've gotten some likes on your page.

Engaging content on your page will compel people to like, comment, and share your posts.

MEMES

The content options work well for the Facebook page include especially content like a meme. Almost every account on the web, both big massive accounts to random social media accounts, always post a meme on their page. So, try to find related memes to your niche and post it. All you just need to do to find a meme is to do a simple Google search. You can also find memes on Pinterest.

INFOGRAPHICS

Another type of content that you can post that will work well and drive traffic to your page is informational content like infographics. These images consist of a picture with some type of writing text over the top of it. To find these kinds of images, all you have to do is to search for things like infographics. Infographics work well for explaining things that have to do with "how to." Alternatively, you can make your own infographic by taking an image to a photo editing software like Photoshop, and then slapping over a text on it to make your own infographic. If you have a website already created, you can even reuse sections of the text on your website and then just paste it into the infographic.

One of the advantages of doing the infographic yourself is that you can also water market it with a link to your social media page, which will bring more eyeballs to your account, as the image gets shared around the web. Another type of content that can work well include stuff are related quotes and related videos. So, start by testing out different types of content on your page to find out what will work best for you, depending on your niche, and then you will find out that certain types of content will work better for you than another type of contents. Once you get a good idea of what is working for you, you can then find and create content that are like those ones that are working well for you.

The goal is to build up enough images and content that will last you through multiple months, and then you can start to cycle to your old content while putting out a little bit of new content here and there. Mini giant social media account of big brands actually does repost the same content multiple times. The trick is just to make sure that you're not reposting the same thing on over two consecutive days, so make sure that you still have enough content so that you can repost a post one month later, and most people won't even notice.

And posting out regular content like this helps in a couple of ways. First, it helps to keep your page and engage up because the more engagement that you're getting on each of your content, the more exposure that Facebook will be able to give you on your future post. So, this means that when you actually post something that has to do with a brand recommendation or has a link, you'll be able to draw more attention to it because of all your posts. And also, this will help with your page organic growth.

Because any time that somebody shares one of your content, their friends will see it in their news feed, and there is a chance that they will like your pitch too. Again, with every piece of content that you post out, you can take advantage of the invite to like feature to view all the people that have liked the post but haven't liked your page. Then you can go through those people and invite everyone to like your page. When you combine all of these strategies, you'll be able to have your first few thousand followers in no time at all.

AUTOMATE YOUR PAGES

The Next step is to automate your pages. So, managing a Facebook page and posting out new content all the time is time-consuming, especially once you have gotten to the point where you have multiple pages and multiple social media accounts. So, there are a lot of tools out there that you can use to take out the headache out of the Facebook page posting so that your content will be able to go out on autopilot, exactly the time that you want.

The FP Traffic tool

And the tool that you can use to manage all your Facebook pages is called FP traffic. Then you can get yourself an FP traffic account. The tool is so effective in managing multiple pages. So, here is how it works. First, you can choose one of the content sources to find niche related images that you want to schedule out from your pages. All you have to do to schedule out each image on your page is to click it, and just like that, it will be added to your page as a schedule.

Alternatively, you can also upload your own image by using the upload images feature, which will allow you to upload up to 100 images on the site. Once you schedule some content on the site, you can then use the scheduled content feature to figure out what time you want the content to go out and also how many times you want to post. It is better to schedule your posts at the times that you know that most of your page visitors will be most active if you created a new page that is closely related to any pitch that you already have before.

The more each post gets re-shared, the more that their friends get to see it, and the more people will like your new pages. If you do this, often, you'll be able to grow your new pages really fast, and your page will become big people enough to attract thousands of likes per post. You can do this without spending an ad. Once you have a big network of niche related pages, you'll be able to grow new pages quite quickly. If you look at most of the big social media account, you will see that they mostly do cross-promotion. If you look at other big social-media accounts, you will see them actually cross-promoting their page with the other pages. Building a network of which pages, and cross-promoting them can allow you to dominate on Facebook.

SET UP A FACEBOOK GROUP

The next step is to set up a Facebook group for your page. Setting up a group for your page can give you another way to post all your content. Groups can be quite viral too and only requires a little push before they start to take off on their own and attract a ton of new members organically.

This will happen as group members start to invite their friends to join the group and as your group begins to show up on the group suggestion on Facebook.

Set up the Facebook Group

To set up a group, just head over to your page, and then choose on the create growth option, and choose a name that is descriptive and related to your niche. For privacy, you can either make your group close or public. It is debatable which type of privacy that you should use in your group. The public option is better, but the closed option will require people to join your group before they can see your content inside of it, which helps to motivate people to join the group.

After you've created the group, you can upload a cover image, and once you are done, you can create a couple of posts on the group so that your group isn't totally empty. To get your first group members, you can just head over to the sidebar where you can then invite people that liked your page to also join your group. And once you have invited a few people, you will start to see your first members joining your group. On top of that, you can also make a post from your Facebook page to your group, telling your Facebook group members to join your group.

If you have a decent number of people on your page, most of them will be able to join your group. And after inviting a few people to join your group and made a few posts on the group, you will find out that you have attracted many group members in your group with very little effort. After that, you can then use your group to reach share content from your pages and also posted links to your other social media account.

Link to other Social Media

The next step is to post that links to your other social media account from your Facebook page. To get the most effect from your links, you want to make sure that each of your social media posts is optimized for Facebook. So, for this, you have to make sure that you have a killer thumbnail and title.

Thumbnail for the Group

Make sure that your thumbnail is simple and eye-catching by using a vector cartoon image for your page. Photo images can work really well too, but just make sure that the subject of the image is eye-catching with facial expressions in it, and make sure that something is intriguing in it. The image that uses can often break or make a post on your Facebook.

You shouldn't create bad images for your Facebook post. Even if your content is good, if you create bad images for your Facebook post that you won't get as much traction as you should. So, make sure that you choose your thumbnail nicely. Then once you've done that, you can then do a Google search for the Facebook debug tool. The Facebook debug tool will allow you to type in your page URL, and then preview how it's going to look on Facebook.

Create Posts on the group

Then if everything looks good, you can just go ahead and post it out from your page. Keep in mind that you will be able to share the post multiple times at your page gurus, so it's a good idea to keep reposting the contents again and again because a lot of the new likes won't have seen it and most people too won't have seen the post the first time you posted it.

You can also post your links out to your related pages so you can post it out on your groups. And your goal is to grow your overall audience to a certain point so that anytime you put out any bit of content, you have turned tons of groups and pages waiting for you to post it out, which will allow you to get a ton of visitors, shares and all that good stuff with each page.

With some of your big and established pages, you'll be able to get tens of thousands of clicks just for one post, and be able to get thousands and thousands of reaches, and thousands and thousands of likes for each post. Having a big network on Facebook pages is very powerful.

HOW TO MAKE MONEY WITH YOUR FACEBOOK PAGE

From your Facebook page, you can average about $200 to $300 per day. Now, most people tell you that making money from a Facebook page is hard because Facebook does not allow you to monetize your traffic, and Facebook continues to make changes to their platform. They tell you that Facebook screws publishers up because the platform does not allow them to get as much traffic from the platform as they were doing five years ago.

So, here is a method for you to monetize a Facebook page.

ADVERTISING

Now, most people will tell you that the best way to make money from the Facebook page is to build a brand or a Facebook group, but if you want to make money directly from Facebook, you'll have to do that through advertising. This does not mean that you will have to sell products on Facebook. All you will do is to make people become engaged with your content so that you can monetize the traffic with adverts. And with this method, you can make about $200 to $300 per day through the Facebook audience network.

If you check Facebook pages like BuzzFeed, you see that they make most of their money from the traffic of the audience that they generate from Facebook. This means that the more traffic they get from Facebook, the more money they're able to make from advertising. It is not complicated to make money from Facebook; all you need is a WordPress blog and a Facebook page. You can start by creating the content yourself initially until you have enough money to start hiring people to create content for your Facebook page.

So, in this section, you will learn how to find the contents to share on your Facebook page and what kind of website or a blog that you will need to make money from this method. You will also find out which tool that you can use to find out which stories are getting a lot of traffic on Facebook, and you can use then use the tool to replicate those viral stories and generate even more traffic from it.

Let's take an example from a big Facebook page like Bored Panda. The page does something very similar to what we are going to be discussing in the section, which is to create a Facebook page that allows you to share viral stories on Facebook. Now, a very bad idea on Facebook will be to try and sell a product on Facebook, because most people are not interested in buying products on Facebook. If they want to buy any product, they can go directly to Amazon or an e-commerce website and buy the products.

So, most people that are claiming that Facebook is a place to sell products are wrong except if they're doing so using Facebook ads. But if you want to make money through Facebook directly, then the best way to do that is by creating content on Facebook, and that is what Bored Panda does. The page has about 40 million likes on Facebook, and they did that by posting viral videos.

If you go down the Bored Panda page, you will find out that they have many videos on their page, and occasionally, they try to post an article on the platform to draw a lot of traffic to their website. The site makes a lot of money when people read the article that they post on their page. If you scroll the page, you will see many articles and videos on their page, because posting videos is the key to growing on Facebook. That is the way you will get likes and get people to interact with your page. There are so many videos on their page, and they post many videos on their daily business page.

Some of the articles they post get about 18,000 likes in 19 hours of them posting it, especially if they post a top article. And with each article that they post on their Facebook page, they can generate about 50,000 to 60,000 visitors to their website.

So, this strategy is all about making money from your Facebook page in conjunction with a news website or a new blog. Now the question is, how do you create a news article or a blog or where you can post about different articles like news and other things.

So, the best way to do that is to register a domain name and use a WordPress plugin to create different categories so that you can upload different content on it. Now you can use a template from theme country to create your WordPress blog. Theme country is a place where you can buy different themes for WordPress.

So, WordPress is the best platform for you to host your blog, because it is cheap, and with a single click, you can install the WordPress theme. You can also decide to buy a WordPress theme or use one of the free themes that they provide for you to create the blog, and in less than one hour, you will have a Blog set up.

FIND CONTENT THAT PEOPLE LIKE TO READ

So now, let's talk about how do you find content that people like to read. Now the best way to do that is to do proper research to find people that are spending money to create content on the platform. Find people who are spending thousands of dollars to create content, and then copy that content, and post it on your page. Now, you're not going to copy and paste what other people are writing.

Still, you are going to take that content and give it your spin, because if you want to make money with advertising, then you shouldn't copy and paste anybody's content so that you will not get a ban from Google or Facebook. You don't want to copy and paste anybody's content or grab an article from a blog to use as your because sooner or later it is going to make you lose your account.

So, what you should do is to go to Daily Mail.com and check their most popular stories sections, where you can see all the videos and articles that have a lot of shares and people talking about it on Facebook.

Now what you want to do is to take the content from the site, add your spin to it, post it on your blog, then sit, and make money from Google AdSense with it. Google AdSense is free to join. All you need to do is to create your website, and once you have a website set up with about 10 to 15 articles, then you can apply for Google AdSense, and they will allow you to monetize your traffic by placing ads on the different sections of your website.

So, you can place different ads on your articles so that when people go to your website either, with a desktop or with a phone, you'll be able to make money when they click on the ad to view it. Now the top way to make money with this method is through signing up for Facebook instant articles. Facebook instant articles are very similar to Google ads, but the Facebook instant articles will pay you for the articles that people view in the Facebook instant app. So, you can post articles on Facebook and make money each time somebody clicks on the article on Facebook, and you also make money from every impression that each of those articles makes.

So, for every 1,000 impressions, you will be able to make about two to three dollars or more depending on the niche or topic that you are talking about. So, the more traffic that you generate within Facebook with your content, the more money you will be able to make. So, if you will generate about 50,000 to 100,000 visitors per day, you can easily make about $200 - $300 dollars or more depending on the topic, and that is exactly what Bored Panda is doing.

If you go to the Facebook app and open up any article from Bored Panda, you will notice that those articles will open inside the Facebook app. Now, Bored Panda is making money from the Facebook instant articles network with those articles that opens up on their page. If you also go to their website, you'll see ads from Google AdSense. You will also see their ad and sponsorship ads. So, to get started, you can grab some articles from the Bored Panda site, add your spin to it, and then post it on your blog. Also, you can find out the content that is generating the most likes and the most engagement on Facebook with different tools.

One of those tools is called Buzzsumo. Buzzsumo is a tool that allows you to analyze multiple Facebook pages. It will tell you which topics are trending in the past 24 hours. It will also tell you the top articles and videos that are generating a lot of engagement on Facebook, which will give you a better idea of what to post about on your page. There are other websites that you can use to track and see how many likes or clicks that those pages are getting on the account, so that you'll know which article to write about inside of Facebook instead of trying to guess what to write about. So, you can also manually track each post to see which ones have the most shares and engagement, and then create content on that.

Now, if you go to The Buzzsumo most shared section and type Bored Panda, you'll be able to see the articles that have more than 30,000 engagement on Facebook. So, this will give you a better idea of what content to write about. And that's exactly what Bored Panda did to get millions of followers.

They created content based on the most trending topics on the internet. So, with the buzzsumo tool, you can go back a week, or even six months, to see the post that has been getting the most Facebook engagement. So, this is a very powerful tool to have in your arsenal if you want to make money on Facebook. Now, this tool is not totally free; it costs about $150 to $300 per month to access it. But it is not recommended that you buy the tool in the beginning. If you are going to invest in this kind of tool, make sure that you have multiple pages on Facebook, and you have a lot of content that you want to produce on different topics. So, you can use the tool to find out what Is working on other pages so that you can try to replicate it on your page.

 If you go to the trending section of the buzzsumo field, you will be able to see what is trending on Facebook at that moment. You will also see what is trending on Twitter, Pinterest, and other social media websites. So, the tool will give you information about what is trending on Facebook and other social media platforms so that you can go out and replicate that content.

Now, if you're hiring a freelancer, all you need to do is to give the person the article so that the freelancer will rewrite it and use different pictures to make the article unique. You can hire a freelancer to rewrite your news articles in places like Upwork or Freelancer.com. You can give the freelancer about 6 to 10 articles per day to rewrite. But in the beginning aspect of creating your Facebook page, you can decide to write all the contents yourself, but remember that it's going to take you some time to make money.

Now the bigger your audience is on Facebook, the easier it is for you to generate traffic. So, when you're creating your Facebook page, try to use a name that is going to fit any category. So, when you're creating your Facebook page, try to use a name that is going to categorize any topic that you want to create. Bored Panda, for instance, does not talk about any specific topic, and they talk about anything that is trending online. So, in the beginning aspect of making money from Facebook, you will need to invest some money into growing your Facebook page into 10,000 to 100,000 likes or more. So, you need to work on your Facebook page daily for it to grow. And when you are getting started, post a lot of videos on your Facebook page so that you can start monetizing the traffic using your website.

CHAPTER 8

How to become famous on Instagram

This section will talk about how to grow on Instagram organically without buying many followers without joining engagement groups. This section is going to show you how to work with Instagram and turn the Instagram algorithm in your favor. As soon as you can make the algorithm work for you instead of against you, then it will be really easy to grow on Instagram.

Don't buy followers

The first step to becoming famous on Instagram is not to buy followers. If you are considering buying Instagram followers, there are many reasons why you shouldn't do it. The truth is that Instagram knows when you buy followers. Instagram have ways of figuring out which accounts are fake, and which accounts are real. All those sites that tell you that they can give you Instagram followers for just a little amount of money and are fake. Instagram is constantly upgrading its platform and eventually, they will know that your account is fake, and most followers will be taken away which would be embarrassing to you.

Also, other influencers will know if you bought followers. People will know that you are buying followers because they can see that your content hasn't changed, but then you are losing followers every day. And then, it'll become very obvious that you are particularly buying followers. Another reason why you don't want to buy followers is the way that Instagram engagement works. It shows your post to a portion of people before showing it to everybody.

So, Instagram will choose about 10% of your followers to show your post before showing it to the rest of your followers. And if that 10% of your followers are bots, then they're not going to show your post to the rest of the people, which means that you are not going to get any actual engagement on your post, and your real followers will not see any of your content. This is not sustainable and is going to be a turn off for you, so it is literally not worth it.

MAKE RECOGNIZABLE CONTENT

The next step is to make recognizable content. Sometimes you will get most of your followers from brand's repost and hashtags, but there are some times that you are going to be able to get more followers on the explore page. The explore page is just a congregation of posts that the algorithm has decided that each Instagram user would be interested in it. And then, by the time people click on your page from the explore page, they will know what you do. This does not mean that you have to become cosplayers, or start recreating characters just to get on the explore page.

The best way to get on the explore page is to do something unique and fantastic. For instance, if you are an illustrator, instead of just doing random illustrations, you can draw someone from a cake pop band. If you're a comic artist, try to recreate meme. If you are a comedian or an actor, then you can do a re-edition of old-time Road. People love this kind of content because people know what it is all about. So, of course, they're going to follow you when you create those kinds of content, because the content is really recognizable. So, whatever your craft is, and whatever you're trying to do, just add a really little flare of pop culture, or an add a moving reference so that people will be able to look at it and know exactly what it is, so that they will be willing to check out the rest of your work.

BECOME A BUSINESS ACCOUNT

The next step is to become a business account. The reason why you want to have a business account is that the account will give you these valuable insights. A business account doesn't just give you the option to put in your occupation, but it also gives you insight into a whole world of numbers that you wouldn't otherwise have on your normal personal account. The most important insights that the business account gives you is the opportunity to go into your inside your feed and find out which post has the strongest impressions.

You can see which posts get the most follows and you can see which post have the largest views. You can see also see which post did well by what month of the year and what week of the year. So, if you are trying to gain some following, then you can go through all your posts and see which posts have gained you the most followers, and that is going to help you to know what kind of post that you should be creating. So, if you are trying to increase your engagement then, you can go through your inside and see which post has the highest number of engagements so that you can create content similar to those ones that have a lot of engagement.

BE CONSISTENT

You will find out when you become an Instagram influencer that once you're consistent, you'll be able to get around 10,000 to 12,000 followers as if you post 12 posts per week, but if you're not consistent and really post twice a week, then you might only gain 2,000 or 3,000 followers that week. Also concerning consistency, you have to have a consistent feed, if your feed is consistently varied, and you have both outfit post and selfies on your feed, then people from your explore page will not be able to know what your account is all about. Even brands and other influencers are going to be confused about what you are or what you care about. Because if people don't know what you are about or what you are trying to achieve with your social media accounts, they are not going to follow you.

Once people are on your page, they will exit out of it out within 4 seconds if their curiosity is not peaked. If you are used to doing colorful backgrounds on your post, then do it for every single one of your posts. One way to be consistent is to have a colorful background on all your post, and then once people land on your page, they will say to themselves that you have very interesting aesthetics. This will end up keeping them a while on your page, and then when they scroll to the top wanting to exit, they will just hit the follow button.

USE YOUR OTHER PLATFORMS TO DRIVE TRAFFIC

One of the biggest platforms that you can use to drive followers to your Instagram pages is Twitter. So anytime that you create something for your Instagram feed, don't just post it on Instagram, also post it on Twitter, and make sure that there is a little caption with it on your Instagram IG. Because most times on Twitter, you will be able to reach people that do not follow you, that is why the post will get a lot of likes, but on Instagram, you can only reach people who follow you, whereas on Twitter, you can reach people that have never heard of you before because of re-tweet. So, if you don't have a Twitter account, be sure to make one so that you can be cross-promoting yourself on your Twitter account. And always tag your Instagram account on all your twitter posts.

USE ALL THE FEATURES OF INSTAGRAM

This means that you have to utilize all the available tools that Instagram has given you. This also means that you have to post on your feed, you have to post stories and you have to go live on Instagram, and you have to do IGTV. Now, this might seem like a lot to do, but the thing is that you don't have to do every single one every day. The Instagram algorithm recognizes when you are using the Instagram platform to its full extent.

So, make sure that you are not ignoring some of the features that Instagram has to offer. If you have never tried out IGTV before, then give it a go. If you have never posted stories on your Instagram feed, then make sure that you will do that. It doesn't take that long to just take a selfie and mention something about your day, create a post, or post a funny picture. Just make sure that on a consistent basis, just as you are posting on your feed, that you are also utilizing the other features of Instagram.

SWITCH UP EVERY ONCE IN A WHILE

If you feel stale on Instagram, then try to post something else. If you are posting the best content in the world, and you find out that the content no longer works for you, then that means that people are getting bored with what you posting. If you find out that your number is tempering off, then try to post something completely different from what you normally post. If you are used to posting costume plays and you find out that your Instagram following is getting stale, and you are not getting any followers on your account, you can switch up your post a little bit and start creating post on costume makeup, and you will see that you'll start to gain more followers again. So, if you are finding that you are getting bored on Instagram, then that means your followers are also getting bored on Instagram, so you need to make them lively.

DO GIVEAWAYS

This does not mean that you should go about promising people giveaways every single day. There are some accounts right now on Instagram that all their followers follow them because of giveaways. Those people that follow Instagram account just because of giveaways are not bots, they are real followers, but they don't actually care about your content outside of getting free stuff. But if you are stuck at 3,000 followers, then you can host a giveaway, and in the comments section, you can say that your followers should repost your photo on their feed.

If you don't want to be that intrusive, then you can tell your followers to talk to their friends in the comment section. And you will be amazed by how quickly, you will be able to break your follower's plateau by just doing a giveaway. However, do not abuse the ability to do giveaway by doing it every month, but just do them for a couple of times per year or even once a year. Not only does this help you to gain many followers, but it also means that you are giving back to people who are supporting you.

Do collaborations

Now don't be afraid to reach out to other artists or content creators that you really admire to collaborate with them. That is how to interact with the people in your industry. Do not be afraid to reach out to people. Most of the collaborations that you will get on Instagram, you are the one who will initiate the collaboration. So, to initiate collaboration, all you have to do is to pick a theme that includes both of you. It's really for both of you to cross-promote each other. It is an example of a win-win situation of gaining followers on Instagram. It is fun to do and it will give you spanking creativity to see what other people do and how you can push yourself. So, there is really nothing to lose with this method and it is really fun to do.

How much money can you make from Instagram

Many people actually want to make money from Instagram, but making money on Instagram solely depends on your number of followers and the type of followers that you have. There are basically two ways to earn from Instagram.

Sponsor posts

This is how a lot of people make money online, especially celebrities and top influencers. Sponsor post is when a brand pays you for posting a sponsored post on your Instagram. Let's use Tom Brady (a golfer) as an example. Let's say that a certain company wants him to promote a certain kind of football or a certain razor, they will probably have an image of Tom Brady using that product, and then he will get paid a certain amount of money for using that product. Now the reason why the ball company wants to pay him for using that product is that he has over 3 million followers on Instagram.

There are 2 main places that will help you to check how much money that you can make for posting an Instagram post as an Instagram influencer.

Inkify

So, to start, go to inkify.com/earnings/Instagram page, and then put in your Instagram handle on the box provided on the website to know how much that you can actually charge for a sponsored posts. So, if you take Tom Brady's Instagram profile and post it on the inkify site, you'll see that Tom's earnings on Instagram is around $17k. You can put in your own handle on the site or put in other people's handle on the site to get an idea of what your goal should be.

Inkify shows that each post on Instagram on Foundr is worth $6.6k per post on Instagram and they have about 1.1 million followers. Foundr really grew their Instagram page by posting quotes and magazine contents.

Sponsoredtweets.com

Another way to make money through Instagram is to use a website called sponsored tweets. You can go to their website at sponsored tweets.com. Now this website allows you to connect with big companies to accept sponsorships. The companies give you an advert to just copy and paste on it your Instagram, and when you post it on your Instagram feed; they will pay you for it. So the first thing that you have to do is to sign in to the site, and once you've signed into the site, go to your profile and go to your connections, you can connect your accounts to them. Then you can go to

Instagram and it will tell you how much each sponsored post on your Instagram will be based on your followers and engagements.

So sponsored tweets and inkifi are two places that you can check out how much your Instagram account is worth, you can compare your account to other account to find the right goal. If you want to grow your Instagram account, then you need to post more tweets, post more quotes and do some videos.

Sell your account completely

Another way to make money from your Instagram account is to sell your Instagram once you hit a certain milestone of followers. If you get good at creating quality content on Instagram and growing followers, then you can be able to build up multiple Instagram accounts and sell them to brands.

Viral accounts

You can sell your Instagram account at viralaccounts.com. Once you're at the website, all you have to do is to go to click on the option, I would love to sell my Instagram account, and then scroll down to the page where it says that you should input your email and the URL of your Instagram account. Then click on the submit button and they will try to help you to sell your Instagram account. Note: You need to have at least 40,000 followers and you can also buy an Instagram account that has a decent amount of following as well, so that you can sell it.

Rev influence

This website is another great place to be able to connect with brands. You can connect with brands like Calvin Klien (clothing), Ipsy, Graze, Grub Hub (food delivery). There are many companies there that you can partner with depending on the type of audience that your Instagram account is targeted to.

CHAPTER 9

HOW TO GET FOLLOWERS ON TIK-TOK

This section will discuss how to get around the algorithm of TiK-Tok.

CREATE VIDEOS BEFOREHAND

Before you actually post a video, create at least four or five videos in your draft. So, as you are recording your videos, you want to make sure that you have some backup to give yourself a break. Once you have about four or five videos beforehand, then you can go ahead and start posting. That means that you will have videos in stock for the entire week. And throughout the week, you will still be recording more videos. So, take one day off to record 4 or 5 videos, and then post those videos once a day. That means you're posting the videos once daily so that you will have a consistent algorithm. If you want to succeed at a faster pace, then try to be posting at least five times a day. It doesn't matter whether a video gets 200 views or 1 million views, just post tons of videos each day, and do not delete anything. It doesn't matter if it has 2,000 views, or 50 views, do not delete any of the videos.

Because people can still be watching videos that you posted about 2 months ago, and that video can still be on the for-you-page. So, post at least a minimum of one video every day. If once per day is too much for you, then try to post at least three to four times a week, but don't post more than once a day if you know that you cannot post more than once in a day, then do not post more than once daily. Do not post two videos on Monday, and then one on Tuesday, and then wait for the next week before you create another video. If you know that you are going to be making three posts in a week, then post them Monday, Thursday, and Friday. You can even create videos and ship-post them.

CREATE A DUET

You can decide to create a duet with anybody. When you create a video that you collaborated with someone, Tik-Tok will probably show that your video to that person's followers. So, you are going to show up on their page. So, create a duet with pages that are similar to yours. Do not create a duet with a cosplay play actor if you are not into cosplay. Do not create a duet with a cosplay actor if you are into organization videos. Do not just create duets with other people, but also engage on their pages. Try to comment on other pages regularly. Take the time to watch their videos in its entirety.

CREATE A POSTING SCHEDULE

Try to post in the morning, before you go to work, which is from 7:30 a.m. to 8:50 a.m., then right before lunchtime at 12 p.m, you can post another video. Then you can post another video between 3 p.m. to 5 p.m if you want to. That is if you have a lot of content, and then do not do anything to the videos until night. Then at night, try to go through all your posts and then comment, like, and respond to other people. If you are a student or you are really busy and your job does not allow you to use your phone during the day, then try to post when you get home at 4 p.m. You don't have to worry about creating a new video every day.

You can even post a video that you recorded a day or two before. Then after you post by 4 p.m., you can then go, eat, clean and do whatever it is that you want to do, if you want to post again, you can then do so at 9 p.m. or 10 pm just right before you go to bed. All it takes is 5 seconds to post. Look at the times that you are posting and make sure that the time is evenly spread apart. Don't make the time that you are posting so close. You don't want to post a video by 8 p.m., then post another one by 9 p.m. It just wouldn't work that way on Tik-Tok. If you're going to be posting three times in a day, then spread out your Post for one in the morning, one in the evening, and then one in the afternoon.

Now, after 15 minutes, do not go back and check your post. Instead, wait until after 30 minutes; the first 30 minutes after posting your video will give you an idea if the video goes viral or not. Sometimes you will not have an idea that your video will go viral in just 30 minutes of posting, but then a few days later, the video will go viral. Also, the 24th hour after posting your video is the most important time to check your videos. The 24th hour is your golden ticket to check your analyst.

Get a checklist to be writing down your video views after the first hour and the 24th hour of the video, because those are the most crucial aspect of your videos. Now the reason why you should record down your views after the 1st and 24th hours of creating a video is because Tik-Tok don't actually give you precise analytics of your video. They don't give you the exact amount of views on your videos. So, if you check after the 1st and 24th hour of creating your video, you will know if the time of creating your video is good for you. If you're going to post in the evening, then post when it is still a bit early, like around 8 p.m., so that you can still respond to comment and go to bed on time.

But if you post late like around 10 p.m. or 11 p.m., then that means she will have to stay awake till midnight trying to respond to comment. Now the first week of being on Tik-Tok is the week where we determine the time that you're going to be posting. And then the second week I've been on Tik-Tok is when you're going to know what your numbers are going to be. At the end of the second week of being on

Tik-Tok, look at the 24th power off at the end of the second week of being on Tik-Tok look at the 24th hour of all your videos to see what your view is like after 24 hours of posting a video.

DON'T DO FOLLOW FOR FOLLOW

If you want to get followers on Tik-Tok, then do not involve yourself in any follows-for-follows or comment-for-comment, kind of thing. The comment for comment is not that bad, the only thing is that you should not be doing it regularly. But the follow-for-follow is a no-go area. If you want to get genuine subscribers on Tik-Tok, then you should try to ignore anything that has to do with follow-for-follow. If somebody wants to follow you, that person should follow you not because you are following that person because it won't look good on TiK-Tok.

It doesn't look too good for your Tik-Tok algorithms and it doesn't look good for your analytics. From the get-go, you need to strive to get followers and genuine commenters. And the way you get genuine followers is to be engaging. If somebody comments on your page, then respond to the person. Try to comment on all the people that commented on your video, at least for that first hour.

Don't make an account to be famous

So, don't go on the Tik-Tok platform because you think you are going to become famous. Do it because you have something just to look back on. When you're starting out on Tik-Tok, do not expect to blow up or become famous overnight. Most times, the video that you think will not go viral is the one that will go viral and get featured on the for-you-page.

Be Unique

Think of some video ideas that's is going to make you unique. Tik-Tok is not like YouTube, where you have to keep creating valuable content. Even if the idea doesn't make sense, just create it because there is not a lot of ways that you can make money on TiK-ToK. Mostly you can really make money on Tik-Tok if you go live or do sponsorships. A lot of people think that if you're just posting about trends like creating a video about a meme that is going viral, then the account will blow up, but that is not the case.

You have fewer chances of being featured on the for-you-page if you create a video about a trend. But you have more chances of getting featured on the for-you-page if you create a video about an original idea where you are giving comedy or singing. The fewer followers you have, the less likely you are to get featured on the for-you-page for creating a video on a popular meme. TiK-ToK will not put you on the for-you-page if other people with more followers than you are doing the exact same video. So, you have to do something unique.

DON'T CREATE A DANCE VIDEO SIMILAR TO EVERYBODY

So, if you are posting a dance video, make sure that you do something different from everybody else. If someone else is creating a dance handwork dance video, you don't want to copy that exact thing. Because that means that you are copying their content, and you're not going to get as many likes as that person, because that person has already made up that dance. So, no matter what your talent is, whether it is dancing, singing, or comedy, do something that was made by you. Even, if you are inspired by somebody else's video, do not just copy that person's video exactly, because it is not going to help you to get featured on the for-you-page.

BE TRENDY

If you go to the for-you-page, you will see many videos that have the same sound. If you see a video that has the same sound, then that means that the sound is trending. If you see a sound that is trending then jump on it and create a video with that sound, because that is the sound that Tick-Tok is promoting.

USE THE #FOR-YOU-PAGE

Whenever you create a video, try to use the hashtag for your page on that video. Because that is what will make your video to get noticed, that is where you want to happen to your content. So, the main trending hashtag on Tik-Tok is #feature-me or #for-you-page. Do not use the #like-for-like because if you do that Tik-Tok will not want to promote your content because you are trying to get bot likes. So, you have a greater chance of getting on the for-you-page by using the hashtag for your page than using a hashtag like #music or #blues, even if you created a blue music video.

TRY NOT TO USE MANY HASHTAGS AT ONCE

If you are creating a dance video, then it's okay if you use the hashtags, #like #dance, and #for-you-page. But if you just insert 1,000 hashtags for your dance video, then Tik-Tok is not going to promote that video because you are basically spamming the platform with hashtags.

DON'T THINK THAT YOU WILL REMAIN FAMOUS

Maintaining the number of followers you have is very hard. It is harder than gaining followers. You can't just post one video today and then wait a week from now before you post another one, because your video is going viral just because you want to keep gaining likes on that video, and you are afraid of that video getting of the #for-you-page.

The reason is that even if you gain a lot of followers from one viral video if you don't create more videos, your new followers will not have any content from you to look up to. Tik-Tok is not a platform whereby if you go viral once, you will keep on going viral repeatedly and have thousands and millions of followers.

HOW TO MAKE MONEY FROM TIK-TOK

In this section, you will learn how to make money from the Tik-Tok app. Unless you are living under a rock or something similar, you should know that Tik-Tok has become a very popular social media app over the last year. The Tik-Tok platform now has become the crease over the internet. A lot of videos on Tik-Tok are now getting millions and hundreds of thousands of views per day on Tik-Tok.

The Tik-Tok app is becoming a very popular app, but the problem is that a lot of people that are using the app are not monetizing it because they don't know how to do it all or they are scared to ask people to buy things from them. Some people have this false belief that they need a large following to make money out of the app like Kim Kardashian. The truth is that you don't need a lot of following to make money from Tik-Tok, even if you have a few thousand followers, you can still monetize that audience to earn some income on the platform.

So, here are some things that you can use to make money with the Tik-Tok app.

REACH OUT TO BRANDS

So if you already have a huge following on the Tik-Tok app, the first thing that you should start doing is to reach out to the brand and let them know about your following, so that you can become a brand ambassador, and promote their product on to your followers. Also, please focus on a particular niche when you are trying to build your following, so that you can easily market niche branded products to your followers. For instance, you can focus on beauty or the gaming niche, and build your followers around that niche so that you can reach out to brands as an influencer to send you their products or give you a paid sponsorship. So, if you have a big audience on Tik-Tok, you can make money by reaching out to brands. As stated before, when trying to reach out to brands, make sure that your audience is solely focused on a specific niche like beauty, gaming, dancing, or comedy.

SELL ECOMMERCE PRODUCTS

Another way to make money on Tik-Tok is to sell your merchandise and services through your e-commerce store. You can set up your e-commerce store through Shopify. You only need about an hour or less to create a Shopify store. Shopify.com is a place where you can create your online e-commerce store and send your product to your followers.

You'll be able to sell physical products and a variety of online products to your followers. You can sell your t-shirt with your designs to your followers.

You can also decide to add your logo to the t-shirt, or design a t-shirt and put all the words that you normally say a lot in your Tik-Tok videos on the t-shirt. Text-based t-shirt sells well online, so you don't need to create any crazy t-shirt design to have any success in T-shirts sales online. If you have a loyal following of people of Tik-Tok, then they'll be willing to support you because you are constantly putting out content, and you have people who are coming to watch you every single day. These people are willing to support you and your inventions, so you need to give them something for them to support you. So, you don't need millions of subscribers to make money from your Tik-Tok following. You can do this with a few hundred or a few thousand followers.

CROSS-PROMOTE YOUR PROFILE ON OTHER SOCIAL MEDIA PLATFORMS:

Another way to make money from Tik-Tok is to cross-promote your profile on other social media platforms. On Tik-Tok, you can start building up your social media channels. If you have a lot of followers on Tik-Tok, you can tell them to follow you on YouTube, because when you start getting more views on your videos as a YouTube partner, you will start to see an increase in your AdSense. Now you are getting more.

If you have any links on your YouTube description or you are promoting any service on YouTube, then sending people over from Tik-Tok to YouTube will increase the views on your YouTube videos. And when those people view your video on YouTube, you'll also get to make more money from AdSense. When those people look in the description of your video, they will be able to see all the products or services that you are offering. And they may also check those products out and buy from the link.

So, you'll be able to generate multiple streams of revenue from promoting your YouTube channel on Tik-Tok. Also, you can tell your Tik-Tok followers to follow you on Instagram and Facebook so that you will be able to make money from the views that you're getting from the Tik-Tok platform. Also, you can create paid retargeting ads to target your fans and your followers on Tik-Tok and promote your merchandise, your services, and any affiliate marketing to them.

So, these are different ways you can monetize your audience on Tik-Tok. So do not create content only on the platform, also try to monetize your audience. Take full advantage of your audience on Tik-Tok. Sell your merchandise and get serious, creating a niche. If you have a channel that is focused on beauty or fashion, it is going to be easier for you to work with brands in the long term. Also, don't rely on the Tik-Tok platform; try to cross-promote your profile, so that your followers will follow you on other social media platforms. And so that you can always monetize the audience in different ways through different platforms. There is so much that you can do with the Tik-Tok app, so don't leave any money on the table. All these are the different ways of making money through Tik-Tok are very easy to do.

CHAPTER 10

HOW TO GET MORE TWITTER FOLLOWERS

In this section, you will learn how to grow your Twitter followers organically without using follow-for-follow strategies or buying bots. Twitter is one of the easiest platforms, to understand among all social media platform, because on the platform, you can get lots of retweets comments, and it's very easy to grow your following very quickly. This section will also show you how to create a Twitter account that gets a lot of engagement and is extremely valuable for people. So, you will learn how to either become an influencer on Twitter or how you can grow an online brand or community on Twitter. So, we are going to talk about how you can generate a lot of engagement on your tweets.

LIKES

The first engagement metric that is going to talk about is likes. Likes are the easiest to get because it takes more effort and endorsements for somebody to respond to tweet you or join a conversation on a tweet that you posted. But likes are something that you can easily get if it is a post about your life or any kind of content on Twitter. So, any kind of tweet you create is likely going to generate a different type of like so far as you have a decent community of people on Twitter. If you engage with somebody on their tweet, the algorithm is more likely to send your tweet out to that person. So, you can get a lot of likes by just engaging with people and joining conversations on their tweets and being a part of the Twitter community. So, you don't really need to post tweets to generate likes; it is going to happen naturally on its own but you do want to post tweets to generate a lot of conversations in the form of comments and re-tweet.

COMMENTS

Comment is easy to get. All you have to do to get comments is to ask a question at the end of your tweet. Some of your most popular tweets will be tweets where you give very little context without talking about your opinions about the question. But, tweets, you're asking and letting others give you their own opinion about the question. The reason why this works is that it helps to generate conversations. So, you want to get your question towards your specific community.

If you are in the twitch community, then make sure that you are asking questions about specific games or streaming in general. This is an easy way to generate many conversations and to get to know a lot of people and allow more people to comment and interact with your content on Twitter. And you should interact and connect with people on their comments as well.

RETWEETS

You will receive retweets if your tweets resonated with people so much, and they want to share it with their community. People are really re-tweeting your content because they are endorsing it, or it's something that resonated well with them. Because everybody that has a Twitter account has a certain number of followers, even if it is 5 people or 500,000 people and all of those people are looking for things to share that is going to be interesting for the people that are following them. So, whenever you're trying to generate more tweets on your tweets, you are doing it by speaking to the audience of the people that are retweeting your content. So, this is a very strange concept to try and understand. If you want to generate more retweets on your tweets, then speak on behalf of a large group of people towards another group of people. Retweets also receive a lot of comments and shares whenever a person retweeting the tweet provides another perspective or value for the community that you are sharing the treat for.

POST CONTENTS THAT WORKS

So, the type of contents that get many retweets on Twitter is content on education, inspiration/motivation, entertainment, and relational. Tweets that are all about generating another relationship or building another relationship between other people don't get a ton of engagement and can clog upon the people's feeds that are you are tagging in those tweets. It's really great to get a lot of comments, likes, and re-tweets around your Twitter account, but there a lot of people that are feeling like you shouldn't be posting things just to get more comments or get more tweets and that is not wrong because in the streaming community, people keep seeing the same tweets over and over again.

You've probably seen or posted this kind of repetitive tweets yourself. Doing so makes Twitter look repetitive and boring. So, you must decide to be the breath of fresh air that other people are looking for in the community. It isn't entirely wrong for you to be creating tweets for likes or for comments, because that is the job of really becoming a content creator. If you want to become a creator, then part of your job is to get your brand across more people on social media. Even if it's tedious to see the same message repeatedly again, you have to remember that it is a way to grow your brand and grow your business.

BE PATIENT

Mastering Twitter or mastering any social media at all is like finally understanding all the concepts of a new game. At the beginning of the game, you be really be confused, and you will have nowhere to go, and you won't be sure of what to do, but then later on, you'll figure it out, and you start winning everyone in the game. So just like every other content creation platform, Twitter takes a lot of time to master. It may take you years for you to get to the point where you are getting a steady amount of comments, followers, re-tweets, and comments and also getting people to want to be your friend and follow you.

The Twitter platform is just like every other platform. In the beginning, it is going to be frustrating because it will look like you are screaming, into the void and nobody is listening to you, but if you can keep at it and keep interacting with other people on the community, then eventually it will come on your way as well. The way to grow your Twitter account to get more followers is to really figure out what it takes to get re-tweets and get people to really care about the things that you are saying. You also have to understand how to format your tweets so that it will look aesthetically pleasing. And that is a big part of social media. And you don't have to reuse hashtags at all, because they are really ugly.

MAKE TWEETS THAT PEOPLE WILL RESPOND TO
First, you have to be able to make tweets that people will actually want to respond to. So, the first step to creating better tweets is to figure out the kind of audience that you want to have, and what that audience is really interested in. If you have a small Twitter account, then you really want to think about who you specifically want to serve and the value that you want those people to get out of your Twitter account. It's really great to kind of niche your Twitter down

the one thing. If your niche may be about people that are trying to pursue their dream and become a streamer, or people that want to learn video game, then the things that you will retreat about will be things that go with that topic that you choose for your niche.

When you're trying to choose a topic, it's really a good idea to have something that ties into the content that you are already creating. If you are already a twitch streamer, then it is something that you should talk about a lot. To find your Twitter niche, you have to think about who you will be to everyone online if you were to make all your content about one thing. Think about something that you are really passionate about because this is something that you are going to be doing consistently over and over. You will literally live and breathe that topic since you'll be creating a lot of content about that topic. So, pick something that you are passionate about and not something that you see others being successful about. Then go from there, and choose a hobby of yours and see who you can become if you create all of your content about that one thing. So, for example if you are passionate about have you cooking stream then that means that you'll be posting recipes on Twitter with great photos and anything that pertains to cooking. If you have an indie game stream, then you could start a long thread about all the indie games that you have played in the past. There are a lot of opportunities on Twitter, but you really need to find your niche depending on what you are passionate about and what you think you can stick with, and also something that you know a lot about, and you can really talk about it forever.

So, the next step is that before you create a tweet, you have to ask yourself who you are tweeting for. So, if this is a tweet that has a lot of strong emotions in it, then it's better that you keep tweeting like that on a personal account. They are many influences that are managing both their influencers accounts and your personal account. Twitter is really a great platform to get your thoughts out there very quickly. So, if you interrupt that niche, then the people that you are already serving will be really thrown off, and those posts will get a lot less engagement, and your account overall will start to suffer.

So, if you find yourself wanting to post about all the random things that happened to you and things that you enjoy without having to worry about your followers and engagement on Twitter, then make a separate account for that, so that you can just say whatever you want. That is a great way to really get your value out of Twitter without messing up the marketability of your professional account.

CONSIDER YOUR ENGAGEMENT METRICS

In every tweet, they are really three ways that people can engage with it. The first one is a retweet, the second one is comment, and the third one is likes. Each of those engagement metrics can really be achieved in different ways. So, to get a retweet, you have to be doing something different from getting comments or just getting likes. So, let's talk about the type of tweets that you must create to achieve this Matrices.

THE COMMENT METRICS

So how do you get somebody to actually comment on what you have created? Most people think that retweeting is a way to show an influencer that you are interested in their company, but commenting on their account is really a good way to connect with other companies because you are showing them that you really care about interacting with the ideas and the things that they are posting.

So, to get people to comment on your tweet, all you have to do is to be conversational. If you're a cooking streamer, then you want to get a bunch of comments on tweets about something related to cooking. So, if you are really dealing with an audience that loves cooking, and loves to see photos of foods, and love to talk about recipes with each other and dining with each other, you can get them to comment on a tweet by being really conversational with them. And asking them questions that will get their ideas flowing and make them feel like you care that they are heard. Also, you could post a photo of something that you really created or a post about your favorite recipe and then include a question asking other people about their favorite recipe.

And it is even better not to include any type of answers in the original tweets. So instead of saying, "I really like this recipe, what's your favorite recipe?," you should just leave it very open for other people to give you their own opinions. So, you should just ask them what their favorite recipe is, and once you are done engaging people, it will become a conversation because you are going to be responding to the comments and telling people about your own recipe. And that is really engaging, because you really have an actual conversation and you will look much more genuine because you are not just telling them about your own recipe, but you are just having a conversation with them. So, in all, just make sure that you are asking relevant questions that your audience can identify with and care about.

THE RETWEET METRICS

So now let's talk about tweets, specifically tweets that have a lot of retweets are usually called viral tweets, and the reason why tweets go viral is that they are extremely relevant to a single group of people who are seeing themselves being reflected in that tweet in a certain way. The tweet can also be a tweet that has a lot of value in it. It could be funny to tweet, it can be an educational tweet, or it can be a news tweet that no one has heard before. In fact, it can be any tweet that can inspire someone.

So, if you include things that are inspirational, motivation, or education in your tweets, then it is much more likely to go viral. So, you want to make sure that whenever you are creating tweets, you are thinking about the specific group of people that you have niche down for. If you want your tweets to be retweeted a lot, then make sure that you are posting tweets that are extremely funny educational or inspiring to other people and for the audience that you have chosen.

LIKES METRICS

The next metric is likes. As stated before, it's extremely easy to get people to like your tweets. People that like your tweets are telling you indirectly that they really like your comments, but they don't like it enough to endorse it.

So now that you know how people engage, how do you put it into practice. First, you have to remember that before you create a tweet, you need to think about your audience and not about yourself. If it is specifically for you, then you have to post it in a separate account. Also, you have to think about what is relevant to the niche of people that you have chosen. You have to ask yourself what is going to motivate and inspire them. You also have to ask yourself what is going to educate and make them laugh. Those things are the things that are going to get you more likes, re-tweets, or engagement.

If you want more comments, also make sure that you are asking questions and being more conversational with that niche of people. As stated before, do not post bad tweets that are all about you. For instance, don't post tweets about the things that you had for lunch, or what you're going to be doing later on, or what game you are going to be playing. Make sure that anything that you talk about that is irrelevant and useful for the audience the niche of people, which you've picked out.

HOW TO MAKE MONEY FROM TWITTER

One way to make money from Twitter is through sponsored tweets. All you need to do is to go to sponsored tweet.com, sign up on the website, set your price for each to tweet, pick your advertisers, and then connect your PayPal account to the website. It's easy to set up. This website is not going to pay you millions of Dollars for each tweet, but it's going to pay you a decent amount of money for making a tweet on your Twitter platform only.

So, you should pick what kind of opportunity you want to promote and the one that you feel your brand is about, or the one that you are interested in tweeting about. Do not tweet about something that sounds ridiculous to you like cars or something weird that doesn't fit you. Try as much as possible to tweet about something that makes sense. The site gives you what to tweet about to make money. All you have to do is to copy it and then add your sponsored link to it, and then when people click on the link, the site will pay you a certain amount.

It may not be a tremendous amount, but as stated before, it's a small amount of cash for you to get comfortable with tweeting through advertisers. So, play around with the site, because it is a cool way to make some extra bucks from Twitter and check out some of the different advertisers that they have. It might even give you an idea of how to pay people to promote your business or whatever it is that you are doing.

REGISTERING ON AN AD OR MEDIA WEBSITE

The first way that you can make money from Twitter is through an ad or media website. The first thing that you need to do is to get an account on the website. All you need to do is to head over and click on the quick sign up button and sign up for an account. Once you are done creating an account, then you can log into the account, on your account dashboard, you will see some options there. If you click on the option of the campaign, you will see the campaign page and an option where it says, you should select your country, select the country that you are. If you're in the United States, click on the United States and then click on the filter campaigns once the campaigns are filtered, head over to the place where it says instant search, and search for Soi. When you search for Soi, you see a bunch of things popping up, and then what you want to do is to click on the American consumer option. Once you do that, it will display an image by the sidebar, and when you click on the image, it will allow you to see the landing page of a website called a cop, which is an American opinion website. The website is going to help you make money by paying you about $1.40 for anybody that you get to enter their email address and password and click on the sign-up button on the website.

ADWORLDMEDIA AND SHRINKEARN

The way to get paid when someone clicks your link and also how to get paid when people sign up on the American consumer opinion website. So, the next step is for you to head back to AdWorldMedia and then go to the option where it displays your short tracking link, all you need to do is to copy the link and then head over to another website called shrinkearn.com. That website is going to pay you some $$$ each time some clicks on your link. All you have to do is to sign up on the account, and then once you are done logging in through the website, enter your username and your password. Once you are done, all you have to do is click on the new sorting link and then paste the URL that you copied from AdWorldMedia click, so that you'll be able to shorten the link.

Now what will happen is that shrinkearn will give you a monitor snake. Copy the link and then head over to your Twitter account and go to the search bar and promote your link to people that are looking for money on Twitter. So, to do that, go to the Twitter search bar and search for the phrase, "I need the money," and Twitter will show you a bunch of tweets that are related to "I need money." Now, click on the latest option for it to display all the latest tweet for the phrase. You will notice that a lot of people are posting so many tweets saying that they need money. You will see people saying that they need money for enjoyment. People were saying that they need money to plait their hair, and even people were saying that they need money to buy a new controller for FIFA 20.

So, there are a bunch of people saying that they need money every minute. So, all you need to do is to like the tweet and then comment on the post with your link.

Now don't spam their post with your link; instead, try to be realistic with them. You could say something like, "Hey I was in the same situation as yours some months ago, looking for money in every way, but I couldn't find any money until I heard about ACOP, so I think you should go check them out with this link," and then, place your link right below their comment. After you've posted the link, you can then comment and allow people to give their opinion on new products. Now once that person clicks on your link, you are first going to make money on the link that you shortened with shrinkearn.com and then once they sign up with ACOP - that is they enter their email address, their password, and when they click on the sign-up button – you're going to make some pennies from the registration.

So, you are going to make $1.50 from the shortearn.com link and 2 Pennies from them registering on the ACOP website. This means for every 1,000 clicks, you are going to make $20 on the ad link website, and out of that one thousand views, many of them will end up signing up on the ACOP website, which means more cash for you. And if you go back to AdWorkMedia.com, you will see a bunch of products that you can promote on Twitter, and then make a lot of money from it. Some products will pay you about $2.03 per click.

They are ones that will pay you $1.40 per click. There are even some that will even pay you over $5 per click. So, the amount of money that you can make with this method is unlimited. Now even if the people that click on the link without signing up with the ACOP, you're still going to earn money once they click on your link.

CHAPTER 11

HOW TO MAKE BECOME FAMOUS ON TWITCH

In this section, you will learn how to grow your stream on Twitch. In this section, we will go through the ins and outs, and also the tips and tricks that every streamer needs to know to grow their channel effectively. If you have been streaming on Twitch, you will know that growing your stream channel can be tough. So, in this section will talk about how to grow your channel and some tips and tricks that most professionals use to boost their stream and their community.

DON'T PAY ATTENTION TO THE NUMBERS

So, the first step to growing your twitch community is not to pay attention to the numbers. There is a very strong reason why you shouldn't concentrate on the numbers, because if you have been putting all your focus into numbers then, you'll not be putting your focus and your attention into your streaming.

So, your streams are not going to be entertaining. If you are concentrating on the numbers, you will continue to feel negative about your vibe, and you'll be wondering why your numbers are not growing but keep on remaining consistent. The truth is that people are going to see that you are not authentic and entertaining because you are only concentrating on the numbers. You are not concentrating on the gameplay, the entertainment, or your community. Also, try not to think of your viewers as numbers; instead, try to treat your viewers as your friends to be in your community. Ask them questions like how their day was, or how their school is, or how is their work. Always ask questions about their lives and show them that you have a stake in them. They will keep coming back if they see that you are building a connection with them.

So, if you can work on the connection with your subscribers, then they will regularly come back to watch your entertainment videos. Even though you are not concentrating on the numbers, you still have to realize that your numbers are still important because if more people chatting or watching your stream, you will be able to have more fun and more energy on the platform. So, numbers are still important. So, you shouldn't totally ignore the numbers, the only thing is that you shouldn't concentrate so much on them. There are many analytic websites that you can use to view your stream stats.

One of those tools is the twitch channel analytic page. There are also many other great websites that will show you how to grow your channel. Those websites will display to you the videos that are the most valuable in your channel so that you can concentrate on creating those types and videos. An example of those websites is the social Blade and Twinge TV.

All of those websites will show you which game is bringing in the most amount of stream views for you. It will show which videos have the highest amount of view count and the best hours for you to upload streaming videos. It will also display your views rate, who gave you the rates, the stream that bumped up your view count.

These things will work to your advantage to help you grow your channel. So, you need to make the numbers work for you. And all these websites will show you which of the videos you are streaming are doing is working well for you at certain hours or times of the day. It will even show you which games currently work well for you on Twitch.

However, you have to use the data that these sites are giving you to your advantage if you want to get the most of out the platform. If you are painting on Twitch.TV, and you noticed that whenever you do black canvas your views skyrockets because people love how the color looks and how it pops up; use that to your advantage.

Whenever you need a surge in views on your channel, paint a black canvas because people will be willing to watch it since they love it watching you paint, and who knows, they might even decide to buy the painting from you after you are done painting it.

LEVERAGE OTHER PLATFORMS

One of the most important advice on growing your twitch views and subscribers is not to start at zero. No matter what channel you have, or what social media platform you are working on, you will start at zero. That means you will have 0 reviews 0 subscribers 0 watch time and 0 everything. But if you are smart, you will learn not to start at zero. If you want to become famous on Twitch, then try to start with a subscriber count above 0. And a way to do that will be to start streaming live. Now you may not have any following or anybody ready to watch your live streaming, but you can invite people from other platforms to come and watch you on Twitch TV.

You can invite your friends from Facebook, Instagram, Twitter, Tik-tok and any social media platform out there to come to watch your stream on Twitch.TV. So, whenever you're doing any live stream, go to other social media platforms that your part of, post it, and let them know which time you are going to be streaming. By doing so, you'll be helping to bump your viewers count above 0, and that will boost your energy and motivation right off the bat.

BRING YOUR FRIENDS AND FAMILY ON BOARD

Now, if you don't have any social media subscribers or social impact on any social media platform like Twitter, Instagram,

YouTube, Snapchat, and Reddit, then you'll have no way of reaching out to anyone out there. In that case, all you need to do is to ask your friends and family to check out your twitch streams. And you'll be surprised that they're going to agree to jump on your twitch channel to watch your game, which will increase the momentum on your channel, and boost up your channel rankings and authorities so that other people can find out your channel. So, don't be afraid to reach out to friends and family to help you out to boost up your views at the beginning of your streaming career.

One thing that you have to note about having friends and family coming into your stream is that they'll help you to create the ice breakers for any new people that come into your channel because they already have some little information about you. They are not afraid to keep the conversation rolling since it is already natural for them to converse with you. So, when somebody comes in, you can easily introduce them to the stream and have a great conversation between them and everyone else in that community.

KEEP ON TALKING
If you've been already streaming and you already have a little bit of a viewer's count, and you noticed that your view count is getting stale and plateaued, the best way to get out of that is to keep your chats constantly moving.

To do that means that you have to talk. Many streamers on Twitch are not doing anything in the stream. When someone says hello to them, they do not say anything back, so you have to learn to talk. Try to come up with anything to say. Talk about what you are doing in the game, talk about your day, talk about what you're going to do tomorrow, talk about what you did yesterday. Talk about your thoughts about the game.

Do anything to keep the conversation flowing, so that when somebody comes into the stream, they are more likely to say, "hello," or make a comment on something that you said within the game. You have to be the one to start the conversation so that somebody will be able to come into your game and say hello. But if you don't say anything back or you are not moving within your chat, there won't be any conversation going on there. Now when somebody comes into your chat and says hello first, try to say something back to the person within 30 seconds to 1 minute. Because most people on the internet have a short attention span, so if you don't reply to their comments within 30 seconds to 1 minute, they will be gone from your channel. So, make sure that you are constantly looking at your chat scrub. You need to look over your chart every 30 seconds while playing your game. Try to get your eyes over there. Put your eyes over your peripheral to check out your chat.

Many twitch streamers don't remember to look at their chat, and that is the main reason why they are not growing. Even if you don't have something interesting to stay, you can always say hello back or ask your viewers how their day was or what their plans are for the weekend. It is very easy to start a conversation only once you can get that snowball rolling.

START A CONVERSATION WITH YOUR VIEWERS

Now getting new subscribers is going to be hard, especially if you're not an engaging person. So, if you're the kind of person that struggles with social conversation, then here are some tips for you to make you come out of your shell and make out on twitch.

TALK ABOUT SOMETHING YOU LOVE

The first tip is to talk about something that you are educated in, or that you're passionate about. Now, this can range from different things. It can be anything from video games to gardening, to working on a car to Engineering. Once you have a passion or you're educated in something, you should be able to tell people more about it and keep them engaged in it.

ASK THEM ABOUT THEIR FAVORITE MOVIES

Another thing that you can do break up the ice with someone in your stream in your channel is to ask them about their favorite 80's movies. And if you do that, you find out that everybody has a favorite movie that they love watching. You can also ask somebody a question about their favorite anime, or movie, or even a TV show to help break the ice breaker. Try to ask a question that you know that everybody will be engaged in or has a favorite something in it. Everybody has a favorite comic book, manga, and video game. Everybody is interested in something, so there's always something that you can find that is going to make that your streamers engaged enough to start a conversation with you.

KEEP IT NATURALLY GOING

So, try as much as possible to keep it naturally going, and you'll be surprised after they have answered your question that everybody in the comment section will jump into the conversation. Before you know it, everybody will start talking with everyone. The next step is not to stream saturated games. A saturated game is a game that you can find in the top 10 list whenever you browse on the twitch game list. So, if you are streaming a saturated game like Fortnite, you will find out that they are other popular streamers with more viewers count than you that is streaming the same game.

So, most people will not want to scroll to find your account to view your game; therefore, people will not be able to find your streaming. So, the best thing to do is to stream a game that is not in the top 10 games and you'll be surprised at how your games will start ranking. So, choose games that are between 11th to 30 games list of games in the rankings. Those games still have a lot of followers and there are a lot of people that still want to play those games. So, try to find your niche in the twitch space. Find games that will help you to get more view counts. Examples of those games are Minecraft, Dark Souls, and Rocket League.

Now, this doesn't mean that you should abandon saturated games. You can still make out one or two days out of your week to play saturated games. In those one or two days, you can play Fortnite and Call of Duty. But the thing is that many people are not going to discover your channel when you're playing saturated games. But that is ok because those days are for you to unwind and de-stress. So, if you remind yourself that those days are for you, then you're not going to be unhappy that most people are not watching or playing with you. So, make sure that even if you choose to stream popular games, you're setting the bar for a certain expectation on what to expect out of the stream, so that you will not have a negative vibe.

WORK ON YOUR LIGHTING, AUDIO, VISUALS, AND AESTHETICS

The next step is to work on your lighting, audio, visuals, and aesthetics. Most times, your viewers' count will suck not because you suck at streaming, it will suck because your lighting, audio, visuals, and aesthetics sucks. All four of these are very important when it comes to streaming. Now, this doesn't mean that your lighting or audio or visuals have to be the best out there. It has to be average. You don't have to acquire expensive equipment, but if you can invest some money into some good equipment, then your lighting and visuals will be great.

Once you get your lighting and Aesthetics right, everything will start to fall into place. A decent light will expose you so that your camera won't work that hard and you won't look very pixelated in the video. Your blacks will look black and your whites will look white. Your face will look crisp and your audio will sound great. The truth is that nobody is going to listen to you if you sound like you are 15 miles away on a space exhibition to the moon. People want to hear a decent and clean audio. And the thing is that the audio doesn't have to be the best, it has to be clean. Nobody wants to hear you breathing into your mic, nor do they want to hear your squirrelly voice.

People don't mind if you are over-expressive, but make sure that you take the time to talk clearly. Also, make sure that you work on your visuals, because visuals are extremely important because that is what will make people engage with your stream people and show up to what you're streaming and what game you are playing. So, if your stream is pixelated or is not coming through or is constantly buffering because your computer can't hold up with it, then people are not going to stick with your stream for a long time.

So, make sure that your visuals are crisp and clean and make sure that your aesthetics looks clean. Make sure that your channel looks clean and that you have good graphics on top of it. Make sure that the channel that people are scrolling to looks crisp and clean. On your channel, try to talk about yourself. Try to talk about how people can donate with you. Make sure that you fill out all the panels that you are supposed to fill because all those things are very important to you. It's not about the streaming all those other kinds of stuff are also going to represent you. So always remember that your lighting, aesthetics, and visuals are very good.

VALUE STREAM COMMUNITY OVER STREAM TEAM

The next step is to value your stream community over your stream team. A stream team makes sense because, it is a combination of streamers that are trying to help each other grow. But the fact remains that it is not true. The streaming community is way better than a stream team. So, try to find friends on Twitch, that you can create a bond with.

Try as much as possible to support them in their journey, also try as much as possible to support them in their journey so that they will support you too. When you are in the stream team, then they are not inclined to help you, but if you can find a stream community, then you will find a group of people that will be willing to help you.

So, when you find a stream community of few friends, try to be part of their channel whenever they are streaming. So, try to find a group of friends that can help to grow your channel and a channel that you can create a community with.

HOW MUCH MONEY CAN YOU MAKE FROM TWITCH

Now twitch streamers have about three different ways to make money from the platform. You can make money from donations, subscriptions, and sponsorship.

THROUGH DONATIONS

So, let's talk about donations first. Making money from donations is very straight forward; all you need to do is to allow your viewers to directly donate to you, with their credit card or PayPal. Sometimes the platform will take a 1% cut, and sometimes they won't take any cut from the donations. You can make up to $2,500 per month with twitch donations. $2,500 per month is on the low side of how much you can make from the twitch donations. it depends on your streams and how interesting they are. You can do this by opening up a PayPal account.

You can open up a PayPal account or a business account to collect donations from your twitch subscribers. Now, what will make you make more money from the monetization is to sign up with an alert service. The most notable alert services are streamlive, stream elements, monkey, or player.me. Any of the above-listed websites work fine. Having an alert service will make the donations a lot more engaging and interactive so that when somebody sends you a donation, a graphic pop up on the screen, which allows you to thank the person who donated to you. And that can even start a snowball effect.

So, it's highly recommended that you signed up with an alert service. Now signing up with PayPal will not cost you anything, but anytime a transaction goes through, PayPal will take a piece of the money because they are a payment processor. So, they charge you a percentage for each money that you make. You can check their F.A.Q. to know how much money they will take from you.

You can even decide to give out your private snapchat to any viewer that wants to donate a certain amount to you. The next way to make money from the Twitch stream is through ads. Whenever you open up a twitch stream, your viewers get to see an ad, and you get to make money from them seeing that ad. All you need to do to activate the ad is to click on the Add button on your dashboard to make your viewers see an ad before they watch your video. You can make a decent amount of money from this method. It is up to you to control how many times you want your viewers to see the ad. You can decide to show a certain ad to your viewers multiple times. So, you can make about $4,000 per month in revenue and that is for showing your viewers an ad once.

THROUGH SUBSCRIPTIONS

The next way to make money from twitch is through subscriptions. Now, this is the most fun part to make money from twitch. You can make your viewers pay about $5 per month for them to subscribe to your channel. The $5 per month is to allow them to get special benefits as your subscribers. So, with the $5 per month in subscription, your subscribers will get a little sub badge and access to so many emoji. If a subscriber pays the $5 per month to your channel, that subscriber will be able to get a dab emoji and a list of other emoji on your channel.

Also, if they pay the $5 per month to your channel, they can choose to set their chat to sub mode only. This means that only people that are subscribers will be able to talk to them. Now keep in mind that you will not be able to keep all that money that you make from this method. Tik-Tok takes about 50% of the money. But if you are a top-tier partner into which then you will keep about 70% of the money which that you'll earn using this method.

This means that 30% will go to twitch, which is about $1.5. A top-tier partner is anyone on Twitch that is averaging about 10,000 views per month. For instance, the number one current twitch subscriber, Ninja, has about 120,000 subscribers displayed on his stream account. If you multiply that subscriber count by $350, you will get about $420,350 per month. The next most popular twitch subscriber is shroud; he has about 42,491 subscribers. So, if you multiply 42,491 subscribers x 3.5 dollars, you will get about $140,000 dollars per month. Now you have to note that not every twitch subscriber is going to pay the $5.

Twitch has something called twitch prime, which every subscriber gets when they link their Amazon Prime account to their twitch account. So those people that link their Prime account to their Amazon account get a free subscription to any channel of their choice for free. So, if someone gets to link their Twitch account to their Amazon Prime account, then they get to subscribe to any twitch Channel for free. So, if you have about four thousand subscribers on Twitch, that means you'll be able to make about $14,000 per month. Now the biggest and the best way to make money from twitch is through sponsorship. Now sponsorship ranges in different ways on Twitch.

THROUGH SPONSORSHIPS

There are some ways that a twitch streamer can get sponsorships. As a twitch streamer, you can get a sponsored stream, a sponsored YouTube video, or a sponsored live appearance at an event. As a twitch streamer, you can also get paid for a sponsored tweet post or a sponsored Instagram post.

A sponsored stream is when a streamer is paid to play a certain game. For instance, Recently, EA Games paid all the top streamers on Twitch to play Battlefield V5. You could tell that EA Games paid the top streamers because they all put the #ad and #sponsored in their title. This is because they are obligated to do so by the FTC, the federal trade commission. The award rate for the sponsored streams ranges from $1 to $10 per year. This means that if you have about ten thousand viewers, you can make anywhere from $1,000 to $10,000 per hour to play a game.

There are times where you will be paid about $10 for each viewer, and any such amount of money depends on how fun the game is and how much money the company has. A mobile game from Asia will have more money than an indie game from steam. Now when someone offers you money to play a game, do not worry too much about how much you are making from the game, instead of to consider whether you're interested in the game or how fun the game is and whether you are interested in playing it. If you find out that a game is trying to offer you about 10000 dollars per hour but the game is not interesting, you can decide to turn down the offer except if they decide to offer you a huge amount of money to play that game.

If you are going to spend about 3 hours of your time playing a certain game, then the money that you're making from that game has to be worth it. So, you need to have realistic expectations when dealing with sponsorship on twitch. Making money on Twitch is fun because you can make more money than people that are working at their 9-5 job for playing bad video games.

Now you can make about $5,000 per video for a twitch 30-second ad on YouTube. Also, you can get paid about $5,000 to $10,000 for every life event that you are invited to. Also, for every sponsorship that you accept, you will have to make a Twitter and Instagram post for it for free because your main platform is not Instagram or Twitter; it is twitch. So, Instagram posts and Twitter posts are added to each deal for free.

Now all these numbers are only going to be possible if you are averaging about ten thousand viewers per month. The numbers are going to be different if you are averaging anything less than $10,000 or if you are averaging anything more than $10,000.

So, if you're averaging about 10000 views per month, you'll be able to make about $20,000 per month from ads, subscribers and donations. If you get any sponsorship on top of that, then that will serve as bonus money for you.

AFFILIATE SALES
The next way to make money from twitch is through affiliate marketing or affiliate sales. All you have to do to make money with affiliate marketing is to sign up with an affiliate platform like Amazon. The cool thing about using

Amazon affiliate is that it's very easy to do, and you can join at any point.

In case you haven't heard of affiliate marketing before - affiliate marketing is essentially when you take a product, put it through a link generator. You get paid each time you talk about that product or send the product to an interested person, and when somebody clicks on the link and makes a purchase, you get a percentage of that sale. So all you have to do is to talk about the product in your content and then mention that you have left the link of the product on your twitch stream, so that anytime somebody goes through and click on the link and purchase the product, you will make a little bit of money.

Now, if you want to take advantage of affiliate sales and marketing, you have to make sure that you make your marketing fits the audience that you are broadcasting to. Make sure that your affiliate products are focused on certain games controllers, monitors, keyboards or mouse that you're using.

If you're constantly producing high-quality content, then don't be afraid to post the affiliate links of your payment supplies. Post the link of the brushes, markers, alcohol inks, and all your payment supplies, because people will be very interested in the product you are using.

MERCHANDISE SALES

The next way to make money from twitch is through merchandise sales. A lot of people think that you need an established brand to start making merchandise sales. But the truth is that you don't have an established brand. You can start from zero because there are a lot of platforms like tee springs design by humans, red bubbles, and more that will allow you to host a marketplace on their site, where you can link to your twitch or any live streaming platform. As long as you produce cool graphics or anything that people find valuable, you can start selling it right away and start making money right off your first stream.

Now merchandise sales can be very tricky especially if you're trying to sell things like stickers or buttons that don't have huge margins on it. However, making a few bucks of each sale is worth it, since it is passive income. So, before you go into merchandise, try to do a little bit of research on it to see if it is going to be worth your time.

**Another way that you can make money through twitch is through e-commerce sales especially if you make a lot of paintings online. But that doesn't mean that you are limited to physical art alone, you can sell digital art too. You could also sell graphic packages or graphics bundles too. All you have to do is to put these things within your streaming channel so that people can know what your prices are and know that you're in a digital artist. Now, if you plan on doing things like e-commerce sales, then try to sign up on any platform that deals with e-commerce like Esty and Wix. Because there are a lot of cases where people have made e-commerce sales without getting their payment or they got some chargebacks. So, WiX and Esty will serve as the middleman to give you that extra protection.

Summary

After you have built a following on social media, the next thing that comes next is how to monetize the audience that you have built on social media. That is what this section is all about. There are two main channels on social media that you can make huge money off as a social media influencer- it is Instagram and YouTube. Don't get me wrong, you can still make money on other social media platforms like Tik-Tok, Facebook, Twitter and the likes, but Instagram is where the bomb is. Instagram is where most influencers make most of their money from, the same as YouTube.

In the book, we focused on how to make money all social media platform especially on Instagram and YouTube and how to make money on both of them. So many people have made their Instagram account a steady source of income for them. If you grow your social media following to a certain extent, you can decide to take it on as a career.

In the book, we talked about ways that you can make money on social media right now from your bedroom. It is going to be super easy and super quick to do. No matter what social media platform you are on Regardless if you're on Twitch YouTube, Facebook, or Twitter. You must learn to monetize the content that you are creating so that you will keep creating that content for the long haul. So, in this section will talk about all the best ways that you can make money on all the social media platforms.

You can make money by creating content on social media, or doing a live stream. Through social media, you can monetize your hobbies, your passions, and your professions. You need to learn how to monetize your content, even if you don't intend to make money on social media.

The money that you make from monetizing your content can be used to buy new software, hardware, games, and other things for content creation.

CONCLUSION

If you want to become famous on social media and become an influencer, then you have to put your heart to it. Do not tell yourself that because you are not getting likes anymore, then you are just going to quit or keep expecting your post for it to go viral. It is not going to happen. So, you definitely have to have the right mindset on social media. You can't just go into social media, and then when one bad thing happens, you quit or back down. Try to copy any trend that you see on social media. The only thing that you have to do is to add your twist to it, especially if the trend is new, because that trend is something that everybody is doing. Because as people are looking through every trending video, they will definitely come across your video, post, or contents. So put your mind to the social media game. Also, try to be following people as you are expecting followers too, because at the end of the day, we are all followers. As stated before, you do not put it in your mind that you are going to get big on any social media platform. Always try to be funny and make people laugh in any little way that you can. Always try to start a scandal whenever you can. Even if what you're doing will not make people laugh, at least let it make people inspired. Also, when you're on social media, expect people to hate you or take you as a joke especially when you will become famous. Becoming famous does not mean that you must be the most attractive boy or girl around. Most of the time, you will become famous because your content is good or because people find you interesting and just want to follow you.

Printed in Great Britain
by Amazon